# When Friendly Dogs Bite

Aggression therapy

for your dog

By Nancy Baer

*2010*

Nancy Baer

Copyright © 2010 Nancy Baer

All rights reserved.

ISBN: 978-1456401504
ISBN-13: 10-1456401505

# When Friendly Dogs Bite

## Chapters

1. Is your dog aggressive toward other dogs? — xiii
2. Does your dog show any aggression toward people? — xlii
3. Does your dog show any aggression toward stranger's? — xci
4. Does your dog have displaced or redirected aggression? — cxx
5. How can you choose a safe dog? — cxxi
6. How can you prevent a dog from biting you or your child? — cxxx

Nancy Baer

# Forward

Kept only in the minds of embarrassed dog owners are the true statistics of how many family pets have bitten. Much in the same way that family abuse is hidden behind smiling faces, many dog owners quietly hold their breath praying that their beloved canine will not bite again.

Your dog may appear to be a friendly, pleasant dog and still bite a person, or fight with another dog or attack the neighbor's cat. You cannot simply label a dog as "mean" or "not mean" and it is not only a stereotypically aggressive breed such as Pitt Bulls or Rottweilers that bite. Any dog is capable of showing aggressive behavior. Many well-behaved family pets have had a growling, snapping or biting incident. The challenging problem is to determine what caused it and how to prevent it from happening again. The goal of this book is to help you understand and resolve the problem.

Understanding dog aggression can be very complicated. Even with our ability to speak and communicate, we don't always understand why humans may have aggressive tendencies. Dogs can't explain whether their aggression is caused by a genetically aggressive parent or it was attacked by another dog when it was only 8 weeks old. Sometimes we are fortunate enough to witness the origin of a dog's aggression. Many times we have to play detective by studying the dog's behavior, determining what the cause is and then attempt to change the behavior.

We must always keep in mind that dogs are animals and their natural reactions are based on their wild heritage. They are very observant and experts at reading body language. Dogs naturally understand human body language which professional actors spend years studying. How many of your dogs know you are leaving your house before you have said anything? They know by the way you move around, look for your keys, pick up your purse or put on your coat. They may know if they get to come along by the clothes you are wearing. Are you wearing work clothes or going for a walk clothes? They can learn that if your expression is angry it is best to stay away until your face looks more inviting.

When a dog comes to me for an aggression problem, I first determine which aggression category they fit into; dog-to-dog aggression, dog to stranger aggression, dog to owner aggression or dog to other animal aggression. In each of these categories there are many sub-categories. This book will explore these different types of aggression to help you understand why your dog is having behavior problems.

Who the dog perceives as the leader of its pack is important information when evaluating why aggression is occurring. For a balanced and safe pack the <u>owners must be the leader.</u>  Dogs look for a leader to be calm, fair and in control. Dogs must feel safe with their leader to prevent fear biting behavior. A leaders job is to protect and discipline the pack. When a dog thinks it is the leader it will perform its job of protecting and disciplining whoever is not following the pack rules. This will lead to aggressive behavior.

A good strong leader does not need to fight, yell or become physical. Often it is about attitude and body posture as you will see in the following true story.

## Magic, Truly Dominant

A true leader does not have to be physical or loud. A true leader does not always need to speak as you will learn from Magic. Magic is an adult male Rottweiler. He was a born leader.

I was working at a large kennel when an intact male yellow lab arrived on the grounds. Thinking he was lost we put him in a kennel, called the number on his tags and informed the owners that we had found their dog. The owners came and got their dog. It was not unusual to have females in season in the kennel, so this lab became a regular visitor. The owners didn't seem to care that their dog was running loose, so we quit calling them.

Our new strategy was to chase him off by yelling at him to go home and making him leave the property. This was a temporary fix. He always returned.

One afternoon the owner of the kennel and myself discussed how we were going to convince this dog that he was not welcome here. "Let's use Magic," she said. A little unsure about how this would all play out we opened the door and let Magic out. Magic walked out in a very self assured manner, sniffed the lab, walked over to the closest tree and lifted his leg. He then walked over to the intruder and arched his head over the labs neck. This yellow lab completely understood what Magic was telling him, he quickly turned and ran off the grounds and never returned.

This is a perfect example of dogs communicating and how a true leader should act. A truly dominant dog does not have to fight. Most fighting and biting comes from fear and insecurity. Fear and insecurity comes from not having confidence in a leader to take care of them. Owners must take the leadership role if they want their dogs to be safe and well behaved.

You don't have to lift your leg on a tree to convince your dog that you are the leader, but there are leadership behaviors we can learn from the dogs. If we use some of their own behavior they will better understand what you are telling them. What dogs look for in a leader is fairly simple. I have broken it down into eight leadership steps.

1. **Leaders go first.** Make sure your dog is the last to go through doors. Not because you are physically holding him back, but because you have taught him/her that they must respect the rules and wait until the rest of the pack goes through.

2. **Leaders eat first.** You should always eat before your dog eats. Picture the wolf. The dominant wolves eat the kill first. You should eat before feeding your dog.

3. **Leaders sleep in the highest, softest, best place.** Your dog should not sleep in your bed. They may sleep on the floor or a dog bed, but not in your bed or on any of your furniture.

4. **Leaders control space.** You being the leader should have control over the space around you and your own body. Your dog should not bump you, jump on you or

lean on you, or step on your feet without you inviting him/her.

5. **Leaders control possessions.** You should have control over all dog toys, food, bones, etc. This means that if your dog respects you as the leader it will allow you to take any item away at any time. Your dog does not have the right to growl or snap to protect the item. However, a fair leader would not constantly be taking things away from its pack. The point is, if the leader really wanted the item it would have the right to take it away.

6. **Leaders control interactions.** The leader of the pack has the right to groom or be groomed as it wants. If you are the leader of your pack you should be able to handle and groom your dog as needed without your dog growling, snapping or biting.

7. **Leaders don't chase.** The leader of the pack likes to be chased. They love taking an item and running with it jut to get the rest of the pack to chase them. Do not chase your dog. Many owners think it is a fun game to chase their dog around the house or yard. It can be fun until the dog has your wallet and takes off with it,or you call your dog to come and it says "Come chase me first".

8. **Leaders are calm, cool and collect.** Leaders must remain calm to keep the pack calm. If the leader is scared or nervous the pack will be scared and nervous. You need to remain calm if you want your dog to be calm. If you are afraid of strange dogs your dog will start showing signs of dog aggression. Anything that stresses you will stress your dog.

So what if your dog is the leader of your pack? No big deal, right? Wrong! I have seen many owners rushed to the emergency room because they allowed their dog to take charge therefore their dog felt the need to correct them. The leader's job is to discipline and protect the pack. Your dog may feel he/she has the right to growl, snap or bite you if you do not take charge. For example; if you disturb a dominant dog while it is sleeping you may get bit. Your dog as the leader may feel it has the right to discipline you. Your dog may feel the need to protect you even if you don't really need protecting. Dogs don't always understand what is happening and may interpret active play as a dangerous situation, resulting in someone getting bitten.

There are some dogs that are so laid-back, confident, and relaxed that the owners can spoil them rotten and the dog would still never think about bitting. Those are the luck pet owners, but most dogs are not like that. They need structure and rules for them to be safe to live with.

Not taking control of your dog can be a very serious and dangerous mistake, as you will see in some of the following true stories. In the following chapters you will be able to determine which type of aggression your dog has.

## Why is there Aggression?

Aggression happens for many reasons most of all natural instincts.

**Genetic Aggression:** Dogs are genetically bred to deal with obstacles in an aggressive way. Their survival is dependent on aggression. Living in the wild they would not eat without killing. Dogs discipline each other using aggression. Growling, snapping and biting keeps the pack in order. Protecting the pack requires aggression.

Some breeds have stronger aggressive genes than others. Dogs bred to guard need to retain their aggressive nature to do their job. Terriers that catch rodents are quick to use their mouths when they become annoyed.

**Dominant aggression:** Someone has to be in charge. Someone in the pack must lead, discipline, and   protect the pack. This dog may use aggression to accomplish those tasks.

**Fear aggression:** An animal that is fearful will use aggression to protect itself. That is survival. Some breeds are less social and tend to be more fearful than others.

**Territorial aggression:** Dogs have a need to protect their territory. Again, going back to survival, a    dogs territory can be as large as the entire neighborhood or as small as the owner's lap. This is not about    protecting the owner because they think the owner is in danger. This is about not allowing another   person or animal to intrude into their space.

**Possessive aggression:** In the wild if a dog is not possessive over its food it well starve to death.
Possessive behavior is a very important part of most animals lives.

# *Chapter one*

## Is your dog aggressive <u>toward other dogs</u>?

My study of the canine pack has revealed a social structure that is intricate and complex. Some canine communication is as effortless as eye contact, yet it can make a very important statement, possibly one important enough to fight over. Some communications are very obvious like teeth baring. Some dog interactions may appear to be harmless play, but are actually behaviors designed to work out the pecking order between two dogs within the pack. A critical part of the dog's social structure is knowing who is more dominant or submissive. To the unexperienced person it may be hard to determine if two dogs are playing, vying for dominance or fighting. This is very important to know or the owner may unknowingly contribute to aggression problems. Interfering too much when dogs are merely playing or working out the pecking order will cause dogs to be confused and frustrated. Hence, aggression starts.

Step one is to determine which type of aggression your dog has from the list below.

**Types of dog-to-dog aggression:**

- *Does your dog growl, bark and/or snap at other dogs within its own pack?*
- *Does your dog bite hard and injure dogs within its pack?*
- *Does your dog growl and/or snap at most strange dogs?*
- *Does your dog growl and bark at strange dogs only when it is on a leash?*
- *Does your dog bite and injure strange dogs?*
- *Is your dog only aggressive to dogs entering its territory?*
- *Is your dog only aggressive when it's behind a barrier?*
- *Is your dog aggressive only when it's paired with another dog?*
- *Is your dog aggressive only to dogs of the same sex?*
- *When your dog sees any another dog does it try to attack?*
- *Is your dog aggressive only to other animals?*

# When Friendly Dogs Bite

## *Does your dog growl, bark and/or snap at other dogs in its own pack?*

In this section we are only talking about how dogs are communicating with other dogs <u>not with people</u>. A dog's pack includes any dog that it lives with or interacts with often. These are dogs that know each other well. Canines have rules in their pack structure. If one dog breaks the rules another dog may show its displeasure. Squabbles over a bone, toy or owners' attention can occur. They communicate by growling, barking or by a quick snap. Normal dog communication may sound vicious to people. Normal dog communication does not include hard injurious bites. An occasional squabble may not be need for concern. Pay attention to the cause and see if you can find a way to prevent it. If the dogs have problems sharing a bone or ball take the items away when they are together. Only allow them to have the item when they are alone. Disputes over the owner's attention is common, but very important for the owners to take control of and not allow this behavior.

Where a dog is resting is very important to the pack order. The leader will not allow another dog to intrude into its space while resting. We have all seen a dog laying down and when another dog gets too close it growls and the approaching dog leaves the area. This is not aggression, this is communication. Other times you may see a dog resting and when another dog approaches it the resting dog gets up and finds another place to lay down. This is also communication. These interactions demonstrate the hierarchy of the pack. At this level it is not aggression.

It is not unusual for a dog to guard its food by growling when another dog approaches. It is saying, "This is my food! Get back", the approaching dog should respectfully retreat. You may avoid this by feeding each dog in its own dish in its own location. As leader of your pack, *you* should not be growled at if you approach your dogs dish. (This subject is addressed in Chapter 2.)

### *Does your dog bite hard and injure dogs in its own pack?*

Dogs that live together and are having fights that cause injuries are a serious problem. Determining the cause of the fight is the first concern. Sometimes the cause is something you can take away or easily change. For example; the dogs only fight when a bone is present. The problem can easily be remedied by not allowing them to have bones when they are together. Whatever the reason for the fights, it is critical that the owners are strong leaders in the household and follow the leadership steps found in the forward.

Dogs work out their pecking order within their pack on a daily basis. It maybe determined by a look or simply a matter of who goes out the door first. It may be stronger body language like mounting, forcing one dog onto its back, one dog arching its neck over the other or taking control of a toy or bone. When two dogs are vying for leadership in the pack, a fight may appear to break out totally unexpectedly but there is always a trigger. Many times the owners are responsible for the leadership struggle between two dogs. They try to be fair and treat each dog equally. Dogs don't understand "equal". They understand pack structure as a pecking order. They need to know who eats first, controls the possessions or gets attention from the owner first. Fighting starts when both dogs think they are entitled to these rights.

The dog that is the most aggressive and does the most harm isn't always the one that starts the altercation.

*If the fighting has gotten to the point that the dogs tense at the sight of each other and no longer trust each other they must no longer live together. Trying to keep these dogs together will cause stress in the house between dogs and owners. Someone will likely get hurt. The following example is a true story to help you understand how serious the fighting can become.*

## "Bobby": A House Divided

As I talked with Joan, a former student and a member of the S.P.O.T. rescue group, a young Golden Retriever limped into the room clumsily dragging his right front leg as he came to greet us. Animal control had found him on the side of a road obviously hit by a car. The shelter had kept him for three days hoping a concerned owner would contact them. When no one claimed this gentle, broken animal, the staff contacted the Golden Retriever Rescue Club. They agreed to pay all vet bills if Joan would board him and tend to his needs. They called him Bobby.

Bobby had suffered a broken shoulder and leg which required major surgery to pin and set the bones. The vet suspected that he might also have suffered some permanent nerve damage making his front leg unusable. He did not attempt to move the leg, in fact, he did not even seem to be aware that it was still attached to his body.

If the dog had any chance of leading some kind of normal life, he would need extended physical therapy. Chris, a good friend, certified massage therapist and specialist in canine rehabilitation. In this world, we all need compassionate, skilled friends. More than anyone, injured dogs without caring owners need them. Knowing Chris' weakness for dogs, I knew she would do all she could to help Bobby. She gladly donated her time and knowledge and took Bobby into her own pack of seven dogs. She spent months massaging and stretching his injured body until he showed only a slight limp on his right side. Chris had worked a miracle, but had also inadvertently created a bit of a monster.

When young dogs suffer serious injuries or illnesses, they require abnormal amounts of nurturing, often for long periods of time. This special, extended attention can change their outlook on life, as well as their view of their "place in the pack". All the attention transformed a very mellow, loving Bobby into a pushy and obnoxiously dominant dog. Jack, the long time resident and alpha male took great offense to the young upstarts attitude.

Inevitably fights began. Most of the fights were over bed privileges and attention from Chris. Those dogs didn't just "discuss" their differences, each wanted to make a believer out of the other. The fights became quite violent. We thoroughly discussed what her options were for her own dogs and Bobby. Bobby would continue to need some regular therapy. He should be placed in a single-dog household with an owner who would bring him in for continued therapy. This sound idea did not solve the immediate problem. Falling in love with this blond beast did not help, Chris made an unemotional decision. She agreed to make every effort to keep the two lead males separated until we found a better situation.

As with many ideas, this one proved easier said than done. One sleepy morning, Bobby followed Chris into her bedroom where his competition lay. Before she could get her eyes open, the battle started. The rest of the pack felt compelled to join in. Chris pushed and pulled the dogs, but couldn't stop the bloody fighting between Bobby and Jack. They didn't welcome her "mediation" and knocked her to the floor. Raging Bobby viciously turned on Chris severely biting her hands and legs. This previously friendly dog had flipped into a non-thinking, biting machine, not caring what or whom he bit, just reacting. Reaching for the bed, Chris grabbed a blanket and threw it over both dogs, disorienting them and enabling her to secure Jack in the adjoining bathroom. Shaken and hurt, she got to the phone and called me.

I arrived to find blood everywhere. Deep red splatters covered the walls, floor, all the dogs, and the phone she had used to call me. Chris had deep punctures in her calf and hands. True to her nature, Chris' first concern was for her dogs. As we examined the dogs we discovered that most of the blood appeared to be hers and Jacks. Bobby had returned to his typical friendly self allowing me to clean him and check his injuries, which seemed to be minor. Jack, on the other hand, would need veterinary attention. More importantly, Chris needed medical attention and quickly.

As the doctor cleaned and stitched Chris' wounds, she and I discussed what to do with Bobby. The situation had changed. He had now bitten and bitten badly. We had more questions than answers. True, he had bitten in the heat of a fierce fight, but would that change him? Would he bite again? How dangerous was he? Could he ever be trusted around other dogs? Could Chris give up on him after the time and love she had invested in his rehab? Bobby's behavior had only exacerbated the problems of finding him a home. At that moment Chris still couldn't think about the "ultimate" option of euthanasia. I took Bobby home to my kennel giving Chris some separation time to consider her choices. While at my place, he reverted to his friendly nature showing no signs of being the enraged beast Chris had witnessed. He did not even seem to associate any of what had happened with her to his behavior.

This devoted lady's decision and proposed solution would stretch most people's imaginations. She knew that Bobby and Jack could never have contact again. She decided to divide her house with a gate giving each male dog his personal territory. They each had their own rooms and own door outside. She would muzzle them if needed. Both would share the household forever separated from one another.

Chris worked hard to make her plan successful, although, she would never want to live this way again and would not recommend it to anyone. The dogs healed. Chris, Bobby, Jack, and the rest of the pack seem content and happy with the arrangement. Three cheers for Chris.

I do not recommend living in a home with two dogs that violently hate each other. One slip and they're at it again. The dogs should be separated into different homes and to be safe, there should not be any other dogs in the house.

### Does your dog growl and/or snap at strange dogs?

It is not unusual for a dog to be friendly and playful with dogs that it is familiar and comfortable with, but to growl or snap at a strange dog. It is often a matter of trust, fear and establishing their place in the pecking order. Dogs have their own way of teaching and communicating. Growling, snapping and baring of teeth can be part of that communication along with an assortment of body postures.

When a dog is relaxing beside its owner and a strange dog enters into its space, a common reaction is for the dog to growl, bare its teeth, snap or lunge aggressively toward the strange dog to say, "This is my space, back off"! If a growl doesn't get the message across, teeth may appear. If the encroaching dog still does not respond a quick lunge and noisy snap may occur. Although this often startles everyone around and usually embarrasses the owner, it is fairly typical dog communication. This action is informing the strange dog that it was not welcome at that point. The snapping lunging dog usually does not want to fight and has found that the startle effect works very well to get the strange dog to leave. This action may even happen if the dogs know each other. A dog that snaps when it is close to the owner may act quite differently when it is loose in a dog park or yard. It very often is willing to participate in play with other dogs off leash.

A happy, friendly, young dog may bound playfully up to a more mature dog and be met with a quick aggressive snarl and snap. The dog that does the snapping is usually blamed for having an aggression problem, but it is the lack of proper dog etiquette on the part of the young dog that caused the problem. The mature dog is giving the younger dog an education on proper greeting procedures. At this point, there is not usually need to be overly concerned. Owners of friendly, playful dogs need to be aware that it is their responsibility to keep their dogs from intruding uninvited into another dog's space. Even though this is usually not a concern, it could be signs that your dog has insecurity, fear or an over protection problem. You do want to discourage such behavior to avoid the action from turning into an aggression problem. Remember that I am only addressing communication between two dogs. Growling, snapping or biting people is never to be allowed.

### *Does your dog bark and lunge toward strange dogs only when it's on a leash?*

Dogs may show a lot of aggression toward strange dogs when walking on leash. They will lunge, barking uncontrollably, as the owners drag the hysterical monster past the strange, dog causing anxiety and embarrassment to the owner. When the next dog is spotted down the sidewalk the owner gets a good grip on the leash, pulls the dog in tight and braces themselves for the next round. The dog has now learned that when the owner tenses up and tightens the leash, it is time to behave like a raving maniac until the strange dog passes. The owner has unknowingly trained their dog to act in this aggressive manner. When the leash is off, this same dog may show no aggression at all toward a strange dog. Many times this dog can go to the dog park and happily play with strange dogs.

This type of problem can be corrected once the owners learn how to handle the leash properly and relax. The habitual routine the owner and dog have formed must be broken. Dogs do not have to act this way! A professional dog trainer should be employed to demonstrate how this is done.

### *Does your dog bite and injure strange dogs?*

Your dog may have begun its aggression in the previous manner and has progressed to actually biting and injuring strange dogs. This of course is a much more serious situation. Unfortunately, we cannot sit dogs down and instruct them to like each other and "play nice". You cannot keep your dog from injuring other dogs unless you prevent attacks from happening. Precautions must be taken to keep this dog away from strange dogs. The owner will need to be relentless about warning people to keep their dogs at a distance. This type of dog should not be let loose around dogs it does not already have a comfortable relationship with. The owner must be conscientious about their responsibility to keep their dog on leash and under control. This dog may be safest at home where it is less likely to meet a strange dog.

Many dogs fitting this category can safely be taken out for walks, but you should employ a dog trainer that has ample experience with dog aggression to help you.

*The following true story is an example of how a bad experience may create a dog aggressive dog. Hopefully you will never be as careless as these dog owners.*

## "Bliss": Attack of the Pit Bulls

I don't often go in search of a dog to add to my personal pack, but this time, I had a mission. I wanted a female puppy that would be a good family pet, perform well in show competitions, to enjoy as a constant companion, and use to breed quality puppies—a big order. A crate full of choices arrived at the airport, nine, eight-week-old Irish Water Spaniels sired by my own dog.

The horde of chocolate brown, energized puppies tumbled out of the crate immediately swarming through my house picking up anything their prickly, little teeth could penetrate. Puppies, puppies everywhere. I began by marking each solid chocolate brown puppy by tying a different colored ribbon on each one. It took little time for the one with the pink ribbon to catch my attention. I couldn't ignore her. She followed me everywhere jubilantly, constantly wagging her tail. If I talked to her, she would leap up and down so excitedly that she frequently rolled over backwards. Totally undeterred, she would scramble to her feet and resume her excited jumping. I had made my choice or perhaps, she had made it for me. I named her "Bliss," a fitting name because of the joy she brought to our lives.

Bliss became my new competition dog. By nine months of age, she had earned her AKC Companion Dog obedience and Breed Championship titles. She evolved into a superb bird dog, adored fieldwork, agility and fly ball. I had no reservations about the quality of puppies she would produce if bred to the right male. The owner of the top male Irish Water Spaniel in the country looked forward to breeding his dog to Bliss hoping to combine the fine qualities of both dogs. Bliss was three years old and he had been anxiously waiting for Bliss to be ready to conceive.

Three weeks after the successful breeding, the county fair opened. As the 4-H dog leader, I parked my motor home on the fairgrounds and stayed for the entire 12-day event. Rising early one warm summer morning, I attached a retractable leash to Bliss and headed out for her "morning constitutional". As she began to take care of business, I spotted two Pit Bulls running full force toward us. Bliss had her back to them and hadn't noticed them. The dogs were intent only on their prey, Bliss.

My mind raced through the options I might have to protect Bliss against the inevitable attack. If I picked up my 60-pound dog, they would simply rip her from my arms. "Think! Think!" I told myself. The oblivious owners of the Pit Bulls were simply walking around the trees when they became aware of the impending attack. The owners raced after their dogs, but they were too late. Crashing into Bliss with full force the Pit Bulls pinned her to the ground and began ripping mouthfuls of hair from her pregnant body. The man reached the rumbling trio and threw himself on them. He managed to grab his dog's collars and pull them up enough for me to pull Bliss from beneath them. The male Pit Bull jerked out of his owner's grasp and charged after Bliss. I put myself between them, grabbed hold of the cord on the Flexi lead and flung Bliss away from the charging dog again and again as if she were a fish on a line. My hands burned from the cord digging into my skin. I could feel my strength weakening. "Get your dog!" I cried, "I can't keep doing this!" Tears were trickling down my face while I kept stepping between the aggressor and Bliss. After what seemed like an eternity, the man finally caught and restrained his dog.

"You have no right to have your dogs off a leash," I ordered.

"They weren't going to hurt her," he responded, gently patting me on the shoulder and ignoring the locks of Bliss's hair still hanging from his dogs' mouths. He simply laughed as though I was an idiot and hadn't seen what his dogs had just done.

"I am a professional dog trainer. I know your dogs were going to kill her and so do you, otherwise, why did you panic when you saw them charging at us?" I blurted. "You don't have a clue what this dog is worth and you had better hope she doesn't lose the puppies she's carrying." Nothing I said concerned him. He smiled and said that I was overreacting.

Realizing that nothing I could say would get through to this careless, irresponsible pet owner, I headed for the fairground police. They searched the grounds, but could find neither the owners or the dogs. I don't want to castigate an entire breed, but Pit Bulls are often dog aggressive. They can present a major threat in the hands of inexperienced, irresponsible owners. Two or more dogs together will often become more aggressive than a single dog. They encourage each other on and instinctively know that they are stronger in a pack.

Fortunately, Bliss's thick coat prevented serious physical damage, but she had bald spots for some time following the attack eventually the chocolate curls grew back, but this experience forever changed her attitude toward strange dogs. Prior to this incident, Bliss had never shown any signs of aggression toward other dogs. Afterward, she wouldn't allow any strange dogs to get within a couple of feet from her without driving them back with a growl or snap. She did not try to hurt the approaching dog, she just wanted it to back away and not intrude into her personal space. No amount of training completely repaired this undesirable behavior. Once she got to know and trust a dog she would show no aggression toward it.

Six weeks after the attack, Bliss gave birth to nine healthy puppies. She went on to achieve the coveted AKC Companion Dog Excellence and Utility Dog obedience titles. Aside from her aversion to strange dogs, she provided us many years of companionship and joy.

### *How can you make a strange dog become part of the pack?*

Assuming your dog is not aggressive once another dog becomes part of its pack, there are steps to help introduce a new dog into the pack. The following steps below should help. The better leader you are the more successful you will be when introducing two dogs together.

If managed correctly, a strange dog can usually join a family with barely a fuss. First, take the dogs for a walk together with two people each having one dog on a leash.

Begin with the people walking between the two dogs so the dogs won't be uncomfortable with each other. It is very important to be relaxed and act casual. The dogs may be comfortable with each other after one long walk or you may need to do this daily for a couple of weeks. Go as slowly as the dogs need before putting them together. Once they seem comfortable, let the dogs walk beside each other with the owners on the outside.

As they become relaxed and comfortable with each other, you can take them into the house. You may want to tie them in the house across the room from each other until they are very comfortable with one another then you may tie them a little closer together. Do not ever tie them close enough to reach each other. If they should fight and get tangled you will have a dangerous situation.

If neither dog has been known to actually injure other dogs and are usually safe with dogs that are part of their pack, you may let them have some time loose in the back yard. If you want to be sure that the dogs cannot hurt each other, you can use the soft basket style muzzles, similar to the ones commonly seen on Greyhounds. If you want to use the muzzles make sure your dog is comfortable wearing it before you turn it loose with another dog. Usually the less the owners interfere, the better. You don't want either of them to get protective or possessive of their owners.

Every dog and situation is a little different, so you must use common sense and good judgment. If the dogs seem tense around each other, then it isn't time to put them together. Some dogs may never enjoy each others company, but most dogs do eventually adapt.

### *Is your dog aggressive only to dogs entering its territory?*

Canines are instinctively territorial animals. They mark and guard their space diligently. If they lived out in the wild, protecting their territory would be crucial to their survival, but in most neighborhoods this is a very undesirable behavior. Many dogs are pleasant and friendly when outside of their marked territory, but when another dog enters its private space it will be met with pronounced opposition.

A dog's territory is probably not going to be the same legal boundaries that are registered at the local courthouse. A dog may consider the neighbor's yard their duty to guard, possibly even from the neighbors themselves. If they are allowed to mark during their routine walk, they may claim that anything encompassing that marked area is theirs to be guarded. Attending a dog park often may give your dog the idea that the park now belongs to him/her. Your dog's perceived territory may be as small as your car, house or back yard, or maybe just its crate or kennel. Although any breed is capable of this behavior, there are some breeds that tend to be much more territorial than others.

To help prevent or fix this issue you need to make it clear to your dog that the territory is not theirs to guard. They need to understand that it belongs to the leader of its pack and you are that leader.

You cannot casually explain to your dog that he/she needs to share the yard with other dogs and must "play nice". Prevention is the best way to avoid problems. Let dogs meet outside of their territories in a neutral location. Once they are comfortable with each other bring them into the territory together.

Do not leave your dog unsupervised in an unfenced yard, allowing your dog to run the neighborhood and claim it as its own territory. Do not leave your dog unsupervised in a fenced yard where it is free to bark at dogs passing by; this will create bad habits. Do not tie your dog in an area where dogs can approach it, this can be very stressful for dogs and it can learn to become quite aggressive in order to get the intruding dog to leave.

**Does your dog show aggression only when behind a barrier?**

If a dog is safely confined behind a fence, house window, in a car, or in its crate, it may turn into a nasty beast if another dog gets too close. Suddenly throwing its body against the barrier, barking, snarling and biting is a very effective way to achieve the dog's goal which is to clear the area quickly. This can be terrifying for anyone near by. They think, "Wow, thankfully that barrier held and the dog didn't get out!" Actually most of these dogs would not have acted that way if they were not safely held behind the fence or car window. Usually, they are worried about the approaching dog and they know that they cannot get away so they do the next best thing which is to chase off the dog. The more startling and scary they act, the faster the intruding dog leaves. This is very common when a dog is in its own crate and another dog comes right up to the gate. The dog in the crate feels safe, yet trapped, so the problem is quickly dealt with by a display of aggression and it works. Dogs have a choice to fight or flight when something scares them. When you take away the flight choice they only have one choice left.

Many dogs show a violent response when behind a barrier, but never show it in other situations. If this is the case, it is not too concerning. However, if the dog does break through the barrier it could continue with its attack. Prevent your dog from being put in this situation in the first place. For example, if your dog is in its crate in a busy area, cover the crate with a blanket so your dog will not see the other dogs. If your dog goes ballistic when a dog gets too close to your car, have him/her in a crate and cover any viewing areas with a towel. If you leave your dog in a fenced yard when you are gone, make sure it is an area where he/she can't see other dogs passing by. A smaller yard behind the house is a good idea. Most dogs will feel much safer and appreciate the time to relax without the worry of chasing intruders.

A dog launching itself against a house window when it sees a dog or animal pass by, may be dealt with in a variety of ways. Yelling at the dog may make your dog think that you are joining in on the assault. One option to consider is not allowing your dog in that room of your house. Only when you are home to supervise you may tie him/her in an area of the room away from the window. Never leave your dog in the problem room when you are not there to supervise. There is a danger of breaking the glass, which may have disastrous results. You need something sudden, yet harmless, to stop the behavior. A squirt with a spray bottle of water or a handful of pebbles in an empty plastic bottle thrown on the floor to make an unexpected noise may be enough to refocus the dog's attention. At that point quickly reward your dog with praise or a treat for stopping. For the treat reward to work you must be away from the window and your dog must leave the window and come to you to get the treat. This will hopefully distract him/her from continuing the barking. The rock throw bottle or water filled spray bottle may also work to stop unwanted barking in other situations.

### *Is your dog only aggressive if it is paired with another dog?*

Dogs are usually bolder when in a pack, they know that there is safety in numbers. This can work in a positive way if you are trying to build confidence in an insecure dog by pairing it with a self-assured dog. This worked very well for me when I brought home a one-year-old Pomeranian that was terrified of other dogs. He would sit in the corner, shaking and drooling, even if a puppy entered the room. He watched closely as my very secure experienced Belgian Sheepdog enjoyed the company of a puppy. My Pom began to follow the Belgian and study her behavior. He found that nothing bad happened and his confidence grew to the level that he now can't even imagine that any dog would hurt him, especially if he is on the skirts of my Belgian.

Unfortunately, some dogs think they are invincible when together in a pack and will take on any other dog. Frequently one dog starts a fight and the other will quickly jump in to help out. The individual dog may not fight when alone, but with the other dog as back up it becomes more courageous. Often owners are devastated to see their dog join in and gang up on a helpless dog that is being attacked. This is the way they would work together if on a hunt in the wild, team-work is necessary for their survival. One dog may take an animal down which triggers the rest of the pack to come help with the kill. I have seen the most mild mannered house pets join in an assault without a thought, just spontaneous instinct. It does not necessarily mean that this dog has a serious dog aggression problem, but to be safe do not pair it with an aggressive dog. You may want to keep your dog away from other more aggressive dogs. If a dog fight does break out the first thing to do is restrain any other dogs from entering into the confrontation. It is much easier to break up two fighting dogs than a gang of dogs.

If you are the owner of two dogs that are ganging up on other dogs, watch carefully and see which dog starts the conflict. You may be surprised to find which dog is the instigator, it may not be the one that appears to be the most vicious. By stopping the instigator you will likely avoid the conflict.

You may have a problem walking two or more dogs together because they become so aggressive that all you can do is hang on and hope they don't pull you over. If this is the case only walk one at a time. While you are walking concentrate on getting your dog to do some obedience along the way. Ask your dog to sit, down and/or stay. Make it clear that your dog must be responsible outside as well as inside. It is much better to have a one block walk in which your dog is well behaved, than to walk for a mile with a dog that is out of control. You may need to attend an obedience class or have a private lesson with an experienced dog trainer. Work with one dog at a time gaining good control of each before attempting to walk them together.

Taking preventive steps is very important! Do not set your dogs up to fail by standing back holding your breath hoping that a fight does not break out. If it is a risky situation, remove your dogs from the vicinity. At least remove the one that usually initiates the trouble. The more experiences your dogs have fighting the better skilled they become. Obedience and prevention are crucial.

**Two dogs packing together can be very serious, as you will see in the following true story.**

### "Sally" and "Sam": Cat Terminators

Walking into the evaluation room, I saw two active Dalmatians attached to colorful nylon leashes that the owners held firmly. The dogs approached me, confidently, anxious to inhale my scent and receive gentle strokes. I obliged them. They wagged their tails and returned to their owners for more stroking. On the face of it, I could see nothing unusual about the dogs, nor could I discern a problem.

The owners prefaced their story with, "These are great dogs". Okay, so what's the problem? There had to be one or they wouldn't have called. Their story unfolded. The dogs, littermates, would viciously attack other animals. They had killed the family cat four months earlier. You can imagine my disbelief when they told me that they had almost immediately adopted another cat which was, as we spoke, at the vet's office fighting for its life. Lisa explained, while constantly petting Sally and Sam, "If they see a cat, they just go crazy wanting to kill it".

I wanted to scream at them."You mean your dogs killed your cat, so you went right out and got another one? Are you idiots, or what?" I managed to keep calm. They already felt bad about the new cat and they didn't need me yelling at them. Keeping a professional tone, I asked if the dogs only targeted cats. Not the case, they explained. Although any cat entering the yard might as well kiss its life goodbye, any other animal received the same "welcome". No amount of speed and intervention stopped the vicious attacks. Sally seemed to initiate the action, but Sam quickly joined her. Lisa and Don explained that they had seen no evidence of aggression toward humans, "just non-human intruders".

Once dogs have killed, they know their own capabilities. Ancient instincts have come to the forefront. Erasing that success from their memories and conditioning them against future acts present almost insurmountable challenges. The chances that these dogs could ever coexist peacefully with cats were next to none. Then comes the logical question, "If a dog is that aggressive toward another animal, what might it do to a child?" Their behavior warrants the question. I have worked with many dogs that behave violently toward other animals. Many do not transfer that aggression to humans, but some do.

Being littermates complicated this situation even more. Littermates spend 24 hours a day together from the time they are born and naturally form a special attachment to and relationship with one another. They have each other so they don't depend strongly on their owners for social needs. Often one littermate will emerge as the unusually dominant one while the other one becomes extremely insecure, which can cause fear-biting problems. Sally, it appeared from Lisa and Don's explanation, dominated and led the attacks; Sam simply followed suit.

Lisa and Don had reached the time when they had to make some decisions and take corrective action. Some of the options did not appeal to them. They recognized that the dogs needed training and that they, themselves, needed to learn how to exercise control over the dogs. Those were foregone conclusions, but that alone would not solve the problem. I suggested that they keep one of the dogs and find another home for the other, because the two dogs together were much more dangerous than one alone. They work together as a pack, egging one another on and giving moral support to keep going. We commonly see children "pack" in the same manner. Three separate, insecure children may behave quite timidly but once they form a group, their behavior changes. Today, we refer to more extreme groups as gangs. As I expected, Lisa bluntly refused to consider separating the dogs. Failing that, I suggested that they separate the dogs from one another, walking and playing with them separately and individually, thus making them less dependent upon each other. They agreed to do that; but none of these plans would guarantee the dogs would be safe around other animals.

    Don and Lisa were looking for a "quick fix", because their new cat was due to come home in a couple of days. Surprised that they would even consider returning the cat to their home, I again stressed the seriousness of having these Dalmatians around other animals. They wanted to keep the cat because of all the money they had invested in saving its life. Frustrated, I virtually ordered them to find their cat another home and never consider bringing it back to their house; doing that would sentence the cat to death. I thought I had made it clear that they could not risk having any animals other than Sally and Sam. Lisa's next comment let me know she had heard, but not listened. She claimed she understood, but said that she did plan to get her son a pet rabbit. "No!" I blurted. "No other animals!" Lisa pouted and said she thought it would be okay because the rabbit would live in a cage. Rabbits get out of cages on their own or with help. Children love to cuddle their pets and sooner or later, Sally and Sam would target the rabbit, which would be no match for the dogs. Not only would the rabbit be torn to bits, their son would have to experience the trauma of that scene.

    Realizing that I needed to be <u>very</u> clear with this family, I again insisted that they install a secure fence, keep Sally and Sam inside it and never bring another animal home. In addition, I reiterated the importance of training so that they would have better control over their dogs.

    Don and Lisa left with their babies, Sally and Sam, knowing what they had to do, but not liking it. The session stayed in my mind for a long time. I just kept thinking, "They adopted a second cat, after their dogs killed the first one!" clearly an example of poor judgment.

## Is your dog only aggressive to dogs of the same sex?

If dogs are going to fight it is more likely that they will not get along with a dog of the same sex, especially if both dogs are unaltered. Most people are aware of the vicious fights that take place

between two un-neutered males, but actually some of the most violent fights can be between two

females. Chances of having same sex altercations will usually be less if your dog is neutered or spayed. You do not need their hormones complicating the situation.

If your male dog plays wonderfully with females, but gets testy with males, you will need to restrict his interaction with male dogs. The same goes for females who don't get along with other females.

If you are living with two males or two females that sporadically have short non-injurious

altercations, you may not need to be too concerned; but if your same sex dogs are injuring each other and are nervous around each other, you must separate them. The best way is to re-home one of them. This type of fighting will tend to happen more often and become increasingly violent to the point that the dogs don't trust each other at all.

You have the most serious aggression if the two dogs will fight when they are left alone. Most fighting happens when owners are present because the owners are part of the reason the dogs fight. Dogs that fight when owners aren't even present must be separated at all times. This is the point of no return.

*Luckily in the following true story the owner was able to rectify the fighting between his two female Jack Russell Terriers before it got to the point of no return.*

### Saved by the Vacuum Cleaner

This clever man was not going to let his dogs manipulate his house and car, so he shrewdly figured out a way to bring them in for me to evaluate their vicious conduct. Sarah and Mandy were two female Jack Russell Terrier littermates that had grown up together. Their owner, Sam, had contacted me when their fighting had gotten so fierce that the dogs could not be in the same room together.

Until both females went into season at the same time they were friendly and enjoyed each other's company. But when the two dogs hit their hormonal peak at the same time "clashing" was an understatement. Once a terrier starts an attack it will go in for the kill. Cuts, blood, stitches, and the vet clinic had become familiar. Both dogs had gone out of season, but so much had already happened that they could not forgive each other. The stress and lack of trust remained.

Sam knew that the two fighting dogs feared one thing worse than each other, the beastly vacuum cleaner. He knew that to save his dogs he must try using it to intervene. No, not sucking them up. That would be a very last resort. He brought the noisy "monster" into the room along with both dogs. In terror they ran around the room too horrified to notice that they were in the room together. They ran. They cried. They pooped. They finally huddled together behind the chair and the beast turned off. This was the first time in weeks that they had touched each other without biting. It wasn't so bad. It was certainly better than that horrible dirt sucker. Sam scooped them up and put them in his car and brought them to me.

Sarah and Mandy showed no sign of aggression toward each other in my evaluation room. I questioned whether Sam really needed me. It seemed as though he had it under control as long as he had the sucking beast on his side. I insisted that he get both dogs spayed right away. I did not hear about any further problems with these two dogs.

I am not saying that literally scaring the poop out of your dog will stop all of its same gender dog aggression, but it shows that there certainly is more than one way to train a dog. This scenario also demonstrates how much hormones do affect dog behavior. If you are not showing your dog in conformation or seriously planning on breeding, do you and your dog a favor and spay or neuter.

**Does your dog charge aggressively after any dog it sees?**

## When Friendly Dogs Bite

If your dog has this type of aggression you will know it. Spotting another dog during a walk will often be enough to trigger this type of dog into an aggressive, barking, lunging, frenzy. This type of aggression will cause a dog to charge through an open door intent on attacking any dog passing by its house. Some dogs have even broken through windows to deal with a strange dog.

I often hear people say, "The dog is only dog aggressive, it is safe with people". This statement assumes that if a dog only attacks other dogs that it is still a safe dog to live with. Shelters are constantly faced with whether or not a dog aggressive dog is safe to place in a new home. If the dog attacks other dogs on sight, it is a very serious problem! Dog fights can be a terrifying thing to watch and especially traumatic if it is your treasured pet that is being mauled. Terrified pet owners often dive in to save their pet and get bitten. Even though the dog didn't intend to bite a human the damage has been done. An incident such as this is devastating to both dogs owners.

Depending on the age, breed and history of the dog the aggressive behavior may not be reversed; but I have been able to turn around some dogs with this behavior if they were young enough and if the reason for the behavior is that they had never been properly socialized. Lack of socialization with other dogs will cause fear of strange dogs. Fear is usually the cause for such aggression. The fearful dog thinks that the other dog is going to hurt him/her so they must get the other dog before it gets them. It seems reasonable that if you can get rid of the fear the problem will go away. Sometimes that will work. Other times we make good progress and then one scary experience with another dog and all your progress disappears. You can not completely erase all the past experiences from their minds. The old behavior can resurface quickly.

The cause of such serious aggression toward other dogs can come from the owner. The owner is either afraid of dogs or is afraid of what their own dog may do if it gets close to another dog. When the owner tenses up the dog becomes alarmed. This scenario continues until the dog is well trained to attack. In this case we can only help the dog by helping the owner. If the owner relaxes, the dog will relax. The owner must gain confidence in the dog and the dog must have full confidence in the owner. Without trusting each other the situation will never improve. You may recognize this type of aggression if your dog behaves differently for different people. They are aggressive when handled by one person and not aggressive when handled by another person.

Do not take this type of dog aggression lightly. This kind of dog needs careful supervision. An exceptionally secure yard or some type of secure enclosure is required. This dog's enclosed area must be in a place where it can't see or hear another dog passing by. Do not tie up the dog. Tying will often cause this type of aggression problem or make it worse. The dog sees another dog approach and knowing it can't get away, it resorts to hostile tactics, lunging and barking. Time after time this aggressive behavior will be reinforced by chasing off approaching dogs. It works! The approaching dog usually takes the hint and leaves. Dog aggression is then born.

The question I am often asked is "Will this dog aggressive dog turn on children?" People are afraid that if a dog will injure another dog it will eventually aim that aggression toward a child. In my many years of training aggressive dogs I have not seen this to be true. Dogs that attack other dogs can tell the difference between a dog and child. Many seriously dog aggressive dogs have never injured a child. Of course, there is the valid concern that a dog could injure a child accidentally during a dog fight. There are of course, some dogs that are aggressive towards people and dogs.

You must contact an experienced trainer/behaviorist to have any hope of controlling a dog with this behavior problem. It is unlikely that the aggression will ever completely be gone.

## *Is your dog only aggressive toward other animals?*

Some dogs show aggression only to other animals such as cats, rodents or farm animals. Their instinct to chase, catch or kill these animals can be very serious depending on where you live. Obviously, if your dog has issues with farm animals and you live in a big city you don't have much of a problem, but if you live on or next to a farm it can be a serious issue. You may think the problem is not too serious if your dog is only aggressive toward cats, but see what the neighbor thinks when they have just lost their precious feline to the jaws of your canine. Dogs have natural instincts to hunt, chase and kill. Their ancestors survival depended on it. Even though our pets no longer need to hunt for their food this desire is still very alive in many dogs. The reflex to chase a moving animal is natural. Fortunately, since most dogs aren't really hungry they don't know what to do when they catch the prey. It is the thrill of the chase that most dogs want.

Obedience training can help prevent dogs from chasing and/or attacking animals, but many dogs still need an added physical restraint, like keeping it on a leash when out in public and having a securely fenced yard. Cats and squirrels have no respect for the dog's own fenced yard and offer dogs their thrill for the day by chasing the intruders. It quickly becomes a game much like kids playing sports. The canine seems to be the only animal that is expected to subdue their natural instinct and be socially correct. Cats can be cats, squirrels can be squirrels, but dogs must be polite.

There are harsh correction devices that can be used to deter the chase and it is up to the individual owner and circumstance to determine whether they should be used. These should only be used under the supervision of an experience trainer.

*The following true story is an unusual display of fly verses dog.*

## Zinger": Dog versus Fly

As this adorable black and white puppy entered my training room, I casually sat in a chair taking care to avoid posing a threat and offered her a flavorful liver treat. Zinger, briskly but gently, took it from my hand and swallowed it.

I often introduce myself in this manner, especially if the owners have reported aggressive behavior or the dog appears to be fearful. I do not want to greet the dog in a challenging, upright position. Offering the dog a scrumptious goody also lets me know how frightened the dog really is. A truly frightened animal will not eat it. If the dog refuses to take the food from my hand, I drop it on the floor and without looking at the dog, begin conversing with the owners while studying the dog's behavior. I continue to drop food closer and closer to me, as the dog becomes comfortable enough to eat it. Occasionally, that specific treat does not tempt the dog and we have to find other lures. Once the dog feels comfortable enough to take food from my hand, I may begin to stroke the dog. Usually, I don't make direct eye contact with the dog at this time. This little Border Collie warmed up quickly with the food approach.

Kathy and Sam reported that Zinger had both aggression toward strangers and obsessive behaviors, which may or may not be connected. Sam had retained Zinger from a litter he had raised, intending to train her to compete in agility trials, a natural "arena" for high-energy, intelligent Border Collies. She was born to work and loved every minute of it. They knew her intensity would be too much for most pet homes. By the time I saw her she had already performed excellently in competitions, but the aggression and specific obsession she had developed compromised her potential, not to mention her charm as a pet. I needed much more information and some demonstrations.

I questioned the owners, at length, about types of aggression and situations that seemed to generate the undesirable reactions. I also needed to know what corrective actions they had taken. They explained that she snapped at people when they approached her in an overbearing manner. Often, people who love dogs don't understand how to approach a strange dog properly and that can cause its own problem. Zinger had also snapped at Kathy who had responded firmly and let the dog know that if she had an iota of intelligence, she would not do that again. That ended the snapping at Kathy, but it did not prevent the snapping at others, especially strangers.

The smallest of the litter, Zinger had shown her demanding side as early as three weeks of age. A person might think that the smallest of a litter might be easier to handle; however, I have often found the smallest to be the toughest. When puppies eat they don't do it politely, giving littermates their turns at the "banquet". Smaller ones must fight to get enough food to survive. If the "runts" continue their "pushy" ways, they will inevitably be a challenge to live with. I needed to understand the root of Zinger's behavior before I could give any instructions on correcting the problem. Did she react out of fear, was she naturally dominant or did she have a physical problem?

As we talked and I continued to study Zinger when a large black fly entered the room. Zinger immediately lost all interest in the food, her owners or me, all she could think of was that fly. Her legs began to quiver and her body tensed. Her intense focus fascinated me. Sam attempted to distract her with a ball, which worked only a moment, then she returned her entire attention to the fly. We decided to end her growing anxiety by resorting to a fly swatter. Zinger watched intently as Sam chased the fly around the room. Wham! The fly met its maker. Sam showed Zinger the dead fly thinking that would end the problem. Instead, she lay down beside the fly, guarding it and making sure it wouldn't go anywhere. Her body still shook with fear of the creature. Every few minutes, she picked it up, bit it and spat it on the floor, as if she wanted to let that fly know she was the victor. Further attempts to distract her worked for only a moment. She returned, again and again to guard that fly. How did they think they could compete in summer agility trials if the dog couldn't concentrate with a fly around? Hello! Flies are everywhere at that time of the year.

Sam decided we had other, more important things to do. He picked up the mangled fly, showed Zinger that he had it, then tossed the fly into the wood stove while Zinger watched carefully. Once she felt certain that the fly had gotten its "just desserts," she bounced enthusiastically and accepted treats. The battle was over and she had won. I still needed answers about what had caused this fly fetish.

"Well, I think it began with our wood stove" Kathy offered. "When we bring wood into the house, we sometimes find hibernating bees that once warm, begin to fly." Sam added that she had fallen into a beehive and had been stung by yellow jackets when she was a puppy. Now on the word "bees," she would jump and bite her rump. He thought that was so funny and he proceeded to demonstrate, "bees" and Zinger promptly reacted.

The fly demonstration told me a lot about this puppy. Being highly intelligent, she had learned her lesson about flying things and didn't plan to experience the pain again. The connection to her other behavior problems may sound like a long, tentative jump to conclusions, but it made sense to me. A controller by nature, she did not trust others, even her owners, to take care of something like a fly; she had to do it herself. If they couldn't do that, how could she expect them to prevent strangers from hurting her? I believed her aggression sprang from fear. She had to take care of herself and was really too young for all that responsibility.

Having dispensed with the fly, we decided to test my theories by observing her reaction to other dogs she didn't know. With Sam holding Zinger firmly by the leash, I brought in Ruby, a hefty, black Belgian Sheepdog. Ruby showed no interest in Zinger, but the little Border Collie launched herself viciously at Ruby, as if she were a mutant fly. A confident, seasoned, five-year-old show dog, Ruby had plenty of experience with people and dogs and felt no threat from this smaller pup.

We moved on to build on the introduction and establish appropriate interaction between the two dogs. I instructed Sam to use Zinger's obedience training and have her lie down and stay, while I walked Ruby around the room. We wanted to let her know what we expected of her. Zinger stayed and watched as I let Ruby run around the room, jumping, playing and receiving pets. We then had Ruby stand still while Zinger sniffed her. Once Zinger became thoroughly familiar with Ruby's scent, she relaxed, laid down and slept peacefully for the first time in our two-hour session. I gave Kathy and Sam instructions on using the leadership steps and to continue the training at home. She felt safe and confident that her owners had the situation under control and the strangers now offered her scrumptious treats.

Kathy and Sam had correctly assessed Zinger's potential for agility trials. She went on to earn many titles in difficult competitions. Most importantly, she gained confidence around strangers and dogs and has ceased to lunge at passing strangers.

With the owners taking control and making it very clear to Zinger that they were taking care of the situation, she was able to relax and begin trusting strange people and dogs.

# *Chapter two*

## Does your dog show any sign of aggression *toward people*?

Dog biting is a very complicated matter. Some common myths about dog aggression are as follows:

- A dog will never bite the hand that feeds him.
- If you love a dog and treat it well, it will never hurt you.
- A dog is only aggressive if someone has been cruel to it.
- A dog is friendly and won't bite if it is wagging its tail

These statements can have some truth in them, but the true fact is that most of the aggression problems I have seen are because the owners have over indulged the dog.

Dogs usually give subtle warning signs that a bite may occur, but many people miss seeing the signals until the dog shows an obvious gesture. This is often shocking to the unaware owners. They think the aggressive act came suddenly with no warning. The fact is there was a warning weeks ago in a similar situation or even seconds before, but no one noticed. The warning may be subtle like muscles tensing, stiffening of the tail, showing the whites of the eye, a low growl, laid back ears or quivering of the lip. It may be more noticeable like a growl, showing of teeth, barking or snapping.

Canine body language can be very complicated even to experienced pet owners. For example, just because a dog lays its ears back does not mean it will bite, it may be showing a submissive non threatening gesture. The tensing of muscles may be because it is physically uncomfortable. One clear warning signal to judge what the dog is thinking would be very helpful, but often not the case. You can be assured that a growl, snap, or baring of teeth is a clear warning that a bite may be coming. Although the baring of teeth can be confused with dogs that get very excited and do a nervous form of a smile.    This can be very confusing to people who don't know this dog's habits.


I have heard many people state that their dogs may growl, show teeth or even snap, but would never bite. I would not bet your home owner's insurance on that. It can be true, but rare. I have seen some dogs muster up the most vicious body language you could imagine, yet never attempt to bite. Don't get your hopes up. This type of dog is one in many thousands.

**If you answer "Yes" to any of the following questions your dog *may* bite.**

- *Does your dog back away fearfully, tail tucked, ears back when a stranger approaches?*
- *Does your dog show the whites of its eyes, tense its body, and hold its tail stiff and high when a stranger or child approaches?*
- *Does your dog growl at people for any reason?*
- *Does your dog bare its teeth at people for any reason?*
- *Does your dog snap at people for any reason?*
- *Does your dog charge at anyone in a forward threatening aggressive manner?*

Although some dogs show these signs and never bite, these are definite warning signs that a dog is uncomfortable with what is happening and a bite could surely occur.

**Lets talk tail.**

If a dog is wagging its tail it must be friendly, NOT! There are several different types of tail wagging and they each mean something different. Let's go over them one at a time:

- Tail raised high and stiff with little movement, wagging only two to three inches from the center, often is a tense, dominant gesture. This is not necessarily a friendly posture. Do not reach down and pet this dog until it relaxes and appears more inviting.

- Tail low, close to or between back legs with fast small wags at the end of the tail, shows that this dog is a little insecure or fearful and doesn't want to make trouble. If this dog is too afraid, it might snap to scare and back off whoever is approaching. Allow this type of dog to approach you, rather than encroaching into its space.

- Larger sweeping tail movement, which may involve the entire body, is usually saying that this dog is confident and welcoming some attention.

## Does your dog growl, bare its teeth, bark, snap, mouth or bite family members?

*Dogs aggressive to family members.*

**Categories:**

- ***Does your dog display dominant behavior?***
- ***Is your dog possessive of resources or hoard stolen objects?***
- ***Does your dog respond aggressively to pain?***

Do not accept excuses for any of these undesirable behaviors "He was tired." "He didn't bite hard." "He was only playing." "He was eating", "He is being gentle when he puts his mouth on me." "He was sound asleep and got disturbed." "She tried to take his bone away." Any of the many other justifications for unacceptable actions are inexcusable.

## When Friendly Dogs Bite

### .Does your dog display dominant behavior ??

Puppies have learned how to interact with their littermates through mouthing, growling, playing tug-of-war, playing chase and keep away games, vying for the best spot in the food dish, getting the best sleeping spot and experimenting with dominant body posturing. When you get your new puppy home, it is your job to educate your puppy. You must let it know that you are not a littermate to play with as it was accustom to. You are the leader and must gently exhibit this. If you have picked the dominant puppy from the litter, this will not always be easy.

Sometimes dogs can be controlling and dominant in very subtle ways and other times the dominant behavior is obvious to anyone who is around the dog for thirty seconds. Subtle signs include, bursting through a door before you, pulling you along on your walk, "marking" all along the walk, stealing your items and running away with them, not coming when you call, jumping on you or climbing all over you. Just because your dog does one or more of these behaviors does not necessarily mean it is dominant, it may just need some obedience training.

More obvious signs of dominance are, growling, mouthing, snapping, baring teeth or of course, biting. If your dog is doing any of these obviously dominant behaviors, it is probably a dominant dog or is being allowed to act in a dominant manner. You may think that is the same thing, but there are many dogs that don't really have a dominant nature and the owners have unintentionally put them in a dominant position. This can actually be very stressful for a dog that is not truly of a dominant temperament. These dogs would prefer not to have to be in control and would be more relaxed if the owners would take over.

**What should I do if I have a dominant puppy or dog?**

With any dog you will want to follow the steps below. If you have a dominant dog, you *must* follow all the steps below and read the "Leader of the Pack" book by Nancy Baer and Steve Duno. Along with this book you should seek the help of an experienced dog trainer in your area to help you with obedience training.

- By twelve weeks old the puppy should know that it is no longer acceptable to put its mouth on any person for any reason. If it puts its mouth on you or anyone, look it firmly in the eye and with a firm voice say "No". If the behavior doesn't stop, you need to leave a leash and collar on and walk it away from whom it is mouthing. You may then tie its leash to a doorknob and let it think about the fact that when it puts its mouth on someone the result was not so fun. Only tie the dog if you are there to supervise and make sure it doesn't get tangled. Once the dog settles down untie it from the doorknob, but leave the leash attached to its collar . If it gets mouthy again, pick up the leash, walk it back to the door and tie it again. If your dog does not learn to quit mouthing, you should seek an experienced trainer to help you. Do not attempt to correct the mouthing by holding its mouth closed, most times this will make a dominant dog angry and it will become more aggressive.

- Do not allow your dog on your bed. Your dog will not have proper respect for you if you allow it to sleep in the best place in the house. Never let a dog sleep in a child's bed. It is hard enough for them to show leadership respect for children without letting them sleep in their bed. On the floor or better yet in a crate (plastic or wire carrier you can purchase in most pet stores) is the best way to start a puppy. Sleeping in a crate will also help with your house training.

- Feed it after you have eaten. The dominant dog gets to eat first and the most. You are now the leader so let your dog watch the family eat and then feed it. You may have to at least make a show of eating a cracker or some small item before feeding your dog.

- Never chase your dog. The favorite way for a dog to control its owners is to steal an object and be chased. Don't do it! If you do, your dog will not have a proper respect for you and it will learn not to come when you call it. It will say, "No, catch me if you can". To avoid this, leave a leash on it and if it tries to run away step on the leash and encourage it to come to you. You may reward with treats and it should always receive lots of praise when it gets to you. This takes the fun out of the "run away" game and makes it more rewarding to come to you. To prevent any accidents only leave a leash attached to your puppy when you are there to supervise.

- Do not allow your dog to go through a doorway before you. In the dog world leaders go first. This simple step can make a huge difference in the way your dog respects you. The first few times you try this it may take awhile to get out the door. Use a leash and don't give up. Make the dog wait until you and anyone in your family goes out first.

- Some good basic obedience is always helpful in gaining respect from your dog. When you speak, your dog needs to listen.

Allowing your puppy or dog to live dominantly in your house can cause a variety of problems. The following stories are examples of several dogs who displayed dominant behaviors. Some were successfully corrected and others could not be turned into safe animals to live with.

*The following story was an aggressive puppy that received early training and leadership and went on to be a very successful companion and show dog.*

## "Casey"

As my daughter's tenth birthday approached, I still had not found her an ideal gift. She only wanted a Golden Retriever puppy, so that she could join the Dog 4-H group. Sounds easy, doesn't it? My husband and I had explained that we already had three dogs and four would just be too many; besides, for my husband's taste one dog is too many. I had decided not to actively search for one, but would consider it if one "came along". Of course, one did.

## When Friendly Dogs Bite

A few days before Jessica's "big day," a Golden Retriever breeder carried an eight-week-old puppy, into my evaluation room. She explained that the buyers had returned the puppy, believing that it had a bad temperament and showed aggression problems. The breeder wanted me to evaluate the dog, which I agreed to do.

After putting this adorable, blond, fluffy puppy through a number of tests, we determined that she probably had a solid temperament but had been taken from her litter too soon. She had not developed proper social skills, such as the all-important, inhibited biting. During the first seven weeks littermates learn from one another. The upshot was that the breeder asked if I would consider taking the puppy or finding it another home. The puppy had "dropped into my lap". After much persuading, my husband accepted the idea that God had provided Jessica's gift and resigned himself to having another dog.

From previous experience, I knew that problem puppies under the age of 12 weeks are fixable. With proper training, this puppy should develop well. Corrective education began immediately. Without saying anything to her, I picked up the puppy, rolled her over and petted her soft, round belly. She snarled viciously and bared her pointy little teeth at my hand. Quickly, I placed my hand under her jaw, stared her straight in the eyes and firmly said "No!" She returned the eye contact, thought for a moment, then began to wag her tail as if to say "Okay, I didn't mean it". Dogs, like children, test the waters and limits many times before being convinced.

During the next few days before Jessica's birthday, the puppy stayed in my training kennel where we worked on her temperament problem. I must admit that several times during those sessions I questioned my decision to give this snappy, little puppy to a bashful, sensitive, ten-year-old girl.

The big day arrived. With Jessica's eyes covered, I brought the puppy into the house and placed her into Jessica's hands. With a big smile on her face, Jessica opened her eyes and hugged her new friend.

"Were you surprised?" I asked, thinking she would be shocked that we had changed our minds and decided to let her have a puppy after all.

"No," she answered confidently. "I knew I would get my Golden Retriever puppy." She truly had the faith of a child that adults strive to have.

She promptly went to work on training Casey. It didn't take long for us to realize that a special relationship between them had developed. I could have searched the finest breeding kennels for years and never have found a more perfect match for her. From the time Jessica accepted Casey into her arms, the dog never showed any aggression.

Casey and Jessica took top honors in many 4-H events. Before long, they had filled Jessica's bedroom with trophies. Several times they won the Grand Champion award in obedience at the county fair. On two occasions, they won the State Championship in advanced obedience. Most years, Casey took first place in agility competitions at the county fair. She also earned her AKC Companion Dog Excellence title, field Working Certificate, and Canine Good Citizen certificate—remarkable achievements for a dog thought to have a poor, aggressive temperament.

Casey lived a very happy twelve years and did more for our shy, little daughter than we could ever have imagined. She truly was a gift beyond measure.

*The following true stories will give you some examples of what it can be like to live with a dominant dog. Not always fun. You may relate or you may be thankful that at least your dog isn't this bad.*

## Yeller

The first time I met Yeller, an unusually large, Yellow Labrador Retriever, he dashed cheerfully into my obedience class towing his owner behind him as she tried desperately to calm him and prevent being drug across the room. I offered Shirley my help and she gratefully handed me the dog's leash. The dog didn't even notice the exchange as he continued his efforts to lunge toward the other dogs in play. Following my standard procedure for curtailing unruly dogs and getting their attention, I gave the leash a firm "pop" and said, "No pulling". Yeller's immediate reaction caught me off guard. He turned around and lunged at me, growling like a Grizzly and gnashing his teeth. I have worked with many Labrador Retrievers, but this one took me by surprise. Fortunately, my quick reflexes and survival instincts took over enabling me to stop him before he made contact. Obviously, Yeller had problems beyond the scope of basic obedience class.

In a subsequent private appointment, Shirley's tale unfolded. She had lovingly raised Yeller from the time he was six weeks old hoping for a "best friend" that would accompany her everywhere.  Even as a puppy, he had displayed some difficult tendencies, but she expected him to outgrow them.  Her first mistake!  She explained that the first real problem came when she attempted to take away a chicken bone he had snatched from the garbage.  She was so stunned by his baring of his teeth and protective behavior of holding his head tightly over the stolen bone that she backed off and let him keep it.  She decided to simply keep the garbage out of his reach.  Shirley felt that she had prompted the incident by trying to take the bone from the dog.  She didn't realize that she had at that moment handed Yeller the leadership role; he now knew he could make her give in and back away by acting aggressively.

As Shirley continued, I heard the familiar story of a dog controlling his family.  Anxious to test his new leadership role, Yeller found other things to steal, tissue from the bathroom, shoes, or books.  He enjoyed this new game and escalated it into other areas.  If she wanted to cross the room, he stood in front of her so that she would have to go around him.  If he happened to be lying down and she disturbed him, he growled and/or bit her.  She had previously contacted a canine behaviorist, but the advice or training had had no effect.  By the time she contacted me, Yeller was three and had bitten her many times.  I explained, "Yeller knows he can get away with biting you and we can't erase that from his mind.  Once an animal has lived as leader of a pack, he will fight heartily to remain in that position.  Yeller is firmly entrenched in that role".  Giving Shirley the benefit of

## When Friendly Dogs Bite

my years of experience working with hundreds of dogs with this same problem, I could not persuade Shirley to save herself and her family and give up on Yeller.

Although I had reservations about the possibility of changing the dog, I agreed to try because Shirley desperately wanted to solve the problem and fulfill the goal that had prompted her to get him in the first place. "I must be sure that I have done everything to save him," she said, through tears.

Our first day of work cast even more doubts about success. When I opened the kennel door, Yeller bounced out joyfully. I attached my leash mindful of our first meeting. We went through basic commands to sit, no pulling on the leash and lying down. He responded happily and well. I thought we might have a chance. Then came the moment for him to return to the kennel. I walked him to his kennel and opened the door through which Yeller walked willingly. I unhooked the leash and started to close the door. He flew at my face with his mouth "open for business". I slammed the door, narrowly escaping attack, while he continued to growl. Again, this dog had caught me off-guard. I had another talk with his owner who explained that while he didn't like going into his crate, he had not behaved aggressively when she returned him to it. I still wasn't sure why he had this reaction when I removed the leash after he was in his six-foot square kennel.

Over a month's time we went through similar routines, Yeller behaving well until the moment I tried to leave him in the kennel. Since that first day, I took extra precautions by using two leashes, one to lead him and one to control him once he had entered the kennel. I took the first leash off and used the other to control the behavior. I tried many techniques to stop his aggressive behavior. He obeyed well until he had to return to the kennel. I tried rewards, but he gulped them and resumed his barking and growling. Correction only caused him to escalate his aggression. I did not relish the job, but I had to tell his owner that she could not safely keep him.

Shirley did not want to give up on him. She took him home and faithfully tried to follow all the leadership steps and obedience commands. After a couple of weeks, she returned to give me the distressing news; he had bitten her bad, and she had opted to have him put to sleep. I noticed her hands were covered with severe, permanent scars that Yeller had inflicted. Embarrassed that I had seen them, she hid her hands in her pockets. "I should have listened to you," she said sheepishly. I do not blame Shirley for wanting to try everything she could to save him so that she knew for sure, without any doubt that she had done the right thing. I do however, have a problem understanding how someone can love a dog so much when the dog is severely abusing them. I have seen this often and because I have not lived in this situation, I have a difficult time comprehending the logic. I think it is complicated because people feel guilty thinking they may have caused the problem.

Although we could not save Yeller, Shirley's story has a happy ending. She had adopted a new dog that showed no aggression what so ever. I have seen her several times since she acquired her new dog. It came to a most appreciative home and continues to be the companion Shirley had sought.

*Some owners would rather live with a problem dog than do what it takes to correct the unwanted behavior. The owners in the following story have chosen to live with the consequences.*

### "Max" and "Joey"

    I greeted an elderly couple as they walked through the door of my evaluation room, each cradling a Lhasa Apso in their arms. They took seats on the sofa holding the dogs in their laps. Soon the dogs left the laps and found themselves seats on the sofa. I already sensed that these dogs enjoyed pampering beyond reason; in this case it was soon revealed to be beyond the realms of safety for others.

    "We need help with our dogs," Vioda announced. "They bite us, our company and anyone they choose. Our friends won't even come over anymore because the dogs attack their feet and ankles when they enter the house." Naturally, I wanted to know what prompted their biting. "Oh, anything. If they are lying on the couch and I walk by too close, one of them will jump up and bite my wrist. They don't just bite, they grab hold and keep biting down. I can hear their teeth grinding on my bones and they won't let go. I can't live this way anymore." She then turned to her husband wanting him to do something to show me how the dogs would bite. I tried to stop him from doing anything that would cause him to get bitten but he ordered one of the dogs off his lap anyway. The dog thought for a moment and then slowly got onto the floor. I held my breath as they stated how surprised they were that the dog had not bitten. At home, that would have surely caused a nasty attack. I explained that since the dog is out of its typical space and routine, it is not comfortable enough to respond normally. I had seen enough. It was time for the grizzly task of exposing the little dictators.

"No, you can't continue to live like this," I agreed. "These dogs need training and you need to know how to take charge of them. They will never be totally safe, but with some work we can lessen the chances of them biting anyone again." Feeling passionately that the owners could not fix the problems by themselves, I urged them to leave the dogs and let me work with them away from the pampered environment they controlled so completely.

She was appalled at the thought of leaving them because she feared that the dogs would not receive food at their usual times. I was astounded! She, her husband, and their friends had experienced punctured ankles and wrists, they lived with defiant, spoiled brats and she wanted to be sure that they would eat on time?! Knowing they would not understand or have the will to follow the complicated training regimen needed, I urged them to leave Max and Joey and let me do the training. Not surprisingly, they flatly refused to consider leaving them and they declined to give their reasons. I wanted to help, but the only alternative they gave me was to instruct them about what they needed to do at home. I was careful not to advise them to do anything that would result in their being bitten, not a simple task under any circumstances and especially difficult under these conditions. A frustrating conversation ensued.

"You must start by keeping the dogs off the furniture," I told them.

"They won't stay off the furniture and if we try to remove them, they will bite us," Vioda responded.

"You will need to put them on leashes and secure the leashes to a door knob so they can't get on the furniture," I instructed.

"Oh, we tried putting collars and leashes on them, once, years ago but they didn't like it, so we removed them," Vioda explained. The dogs were always carried if they needed to go somewhere. I could hardly believe that the owners surrendered to the dogs every demand. We would have a world unfit for habitation if all parents raised their children this way. While I understand some of the reasons, I cannot relate to people who willing give control to their dogs and abdicate responsibility for their pets' behaviors.

Vioda and Ray wanted two dogs they could love and spoil. Unfortunately, Max and Joey were not the dogs for that. The dogs clearly had stronger wills than their owners. I begged them to let me keep one of the dogs thinking I might be able to ease them into the idea of training. If I could have gotten the dogs accustomed to a leash and collar and given them some obedience training, even one at a time, I might have lessened the biting risk and made them more respectable citizens. Vioda just repeated her concern about their being fed on time. They left with Ray scooping Joey into his arms simply saying, "We'll think about it."

After they left, I remained in the evaluation room, horrified at what I had witnessed and wondering what I could have done. I have no answers if people refuse to take control. I have had no further contact. If Vioda and Ray took no action, they live isolated from friends, as prisoners and servants of two ungrateful dogs.

*Sometimes a dog simply ends up mismatched with the family. A personality clash between canine and owner can become quite serious. The following dog was very fortunate that after some bad matches, he finally found the perfect home to live out his long life.*

## Casper

"He is a monster in a Sheltie's body, we wish we had never met him!" read the first sentence in a six-page letter that arrived with the high-strung Shetland Sheep Dog. Casper had been found loose on the streets, was turned over to Seattle Purebred Dog Rescue (SPDR), then adopted by a family with two children, the family that had sent the letter.

Casper did have some neurotic behaviors. On cue, his herding instinct kicked into high gear. Anything that got the family moving ignited his herding drive. The phones ringing caused people to move. When people moved, he chased them and bit their ankles. What fun for this active little dog! Doorbells and microwave dings provided equal stimulation. If the family did not move fast enough, his genetic duty compelled him to nip harder, in an effort to control his herd of people. Given the frequency of these cues, the family had punctured, bleeding ankles.

The family misunderstood and mistakenly concluded that he must be afraid of the telephone, doorbell and microwave. They did the logical thing based on their assumptions; they held and petted him, trying to reassure him that it was okay and they would keep him safe. They held him on their laps to comfort him. This only reinforced his behavior and made him more anxious to get them moving, so he would bite them. Frustrated, the family contacted a canine behaviorist who assessed the problem to be a leadership issue. Casper was controlling the family, fear was not the problem. She instructed them to do an "alpha roll". When the dog went into action, they were to grab him suddenly and roll him on his back while yelling about how bad he was. Thinking his "herd" was rebelling, Casper intensified his efforts by biting even harder. To make matters worse, the next time the family responded to the doorbell he took special care to stay out of their reach.

They could not even take the dog for walks because passing cars galvanized Casper into action. He would spin in circles barking hysterically, while his owners held on tightly to the leash. The situation had reached an impasse, and he was returned to SPDR, who fostered him temporarily with a friend of mine. Toni called me, asking if I would be willing to work with Casper. I could barely hear her talking to me because Casper was running circles around her barking, and she could not make him stop. He became an "exhibit" and training project in one of my dog trainer classes.

Little Casper was now introduced to Boot Camp, and for any dog, it begins with basic obedience training and respect. If a dog refuses to follow basic commands, further training will fail. Casper earned his stripes admirably. Throughout this phase, he remained friendly and responsive. We saw no signs of the reported aggression, but I was certain that it lurked in yet undiscovered crannies. Feeling sure he had heard and learned to ignore most correction words, I introduced another type of sound correction developed by John Fisher called "Discs". The tool consists of five, round, metal discs placed on a string similar to a key ring. They make a clanging sound when dropped on the floor. Carefully using John's program of using food to condition this clanging sound as a sign to stop what he was doing worked splendidly with Casper. We were, in effect, able to reverse his conditioning. Instead of going into action, the dog learned to stop when the discs hit the floor.

    Next, we tackled the car-chasing problem. Building on the foundation we had laid and employing the discs, we ventured onto a busy street. Watching those cars whizzing down the highways made Casper's body trembled with excitement. Barks burst from his mouth and he spun violently in circles at the end of the leash, but the sound of the dropped discs stopped him instantly. I insisted that he sit quietly for a short time as the cars passed by. It took all the restraint and self-control he could muster. My students took turns walking him up and down the road punctuating the walk with basic commands. We did allow him a small bit of whining, after all, this was a big behavior change for him. Another victory chalked up.

    We moved to the final task, the telephone. I don't usually integrate foster dogs into my house pack, but this training required it. With two phone lines to the house, we could easily stage phone-ringing sessions. First, we just let the phone ring. When nobody went to answer it, Casper became confused, running in circles and whining not knowing what we expected him to do. If he barked at the phone, we dropped the discs. This stopped him immediately, and he would go lie down. Next, we attached a leash; and a person walked toward the ringing phone. If Casper moved toward the person, I said "No" and stepped on the leash to stop him. If he ran and barked, I dropped the discs. Finally, we took aim at his drive to chase something moving fast. I loosely held the leash and discs while someone ran toward the ringing phone. When Casper moved toward the person, I said "No" and either pulled on the leash or dropped the discs. We needed only a couple of runs for him to get the point and comply.

Casper was now ready to be placed in a home where the training would be continued. If he went to a home where people didn't understand him or spoiled him, he could quickly return to being the monster he had been. My eight-year-old granddaughter, Autumn, she had become attached to Casper, during his two-month stay at our house. She had recently joined Dog 4-H and needed a dog to show. After much consideration we agreed to let her try.

Casper got used to spending so much time in the house he thought he was now part of our family. Autumn returned him to the kennel one evening and Casper angrily grabbed Autumns coat sleeve, implying that he did not think he deserved to be one of the kennel dogs. Autumn being raised in a house of dog trainers responded quickly and firmly. With a low stern voice and firm direct eye contact she told Casper "No"! She then, in true trainer form, removed Casper from the kennel and put him back in several times so that she could get the point across to him that *she* had the right to put him in the kennel, and he did not have the right to put his mouth on her for any reason. That was the last time he ever challenged her. Had she not passed the test of this kennel challenge, she would not have been able to take him on as her own special dog. She has been showing him for several years in county and state fairs.

We only smile when Autumn is asked were she got such a wonderful Sheltie. He is totally devoted to her and will happily do anything for her. They have a room filled with trophies and ribbons. Love, understanding, consistency and training transformed this little dog into a child's dream.

## Does your dog act possessive over resources or hoard stolen objects?

Many owners get bitten just for taking a tissue that was stolen from a wastebasket away from their dog. This is one of the most serious types of aggression and unfortunately all too common. Some of these dogs are possessive over food, but most become abnormally violent when they have stolen something. It doesn't really matter what is stolen, it is just the act of stealing that triggers a possessive reaction. Sometimes the person is unaware that the dog is protecting a plundered possession and is swiftly bitten just for getting too close.

These dogs are rarely possessive over their own toys because the toys are already theirs. Many of these dogs have food whenever they want it, so there is no fun in possessing that. They usually get excited about what seems to be most important to the owners. They keep searching the house until they find that thing that will get the owners attention, then they play the keep-away game. The game becomes more and more serious with growling, baring teeth, posturing over the item and then a snap. If that works the next step is a bite, that may not be hard at first, just a scratch on the skin or light bruise. The next time the bite comes quicker and is much harder.

# When Friendly Dogs Bite

*The following true story is one I personally lived with. I took her on as a young puppy to see if I could modify her aggressive behavior and make her safe to live with.*

## "Challenger"

I can boast of consistent success in making a safe, dependable dog out of any puppy if I can work with the puppy while it is under 12 weeks of age. While many older dogs can be trained, they present greater challenges because, among other things, I must erase old habits and memories the dog has of past "victories" and experiences.

Life in a litter involves biting games that become part of a puppy's memories. They continue these biting games when they go into their new human homes. Ideally, by the age of 12 weeks, a puppy should have learned that it is not acceptable to put its mouth on people in an angry manner. Many owners wait too long to start training, hoping the puppy will simply outgrow the improper biting behavior.

At 16 weeks, Challenger did not have a glimmer of respect for people, and felt she had the prerogative to chomp firmly on anyone who annoyed her. Being novice dog owners, Harvey and Theresa had concerned themselves largely with making Challenger happy by spoiling her rotten and creating a biting monster. By the time I met them, both had the memory of Challenger permanently scarred on their hands.

As Harvey and Theresa entered my evaluation room, "towed" by Challenger, I studied them carefully. A young dog entering new, unfamiliar territory will often sniff around cautiously and check to see if her owners seem comfortable with the situation and me. Some will put on the "brakes" and need to be carried into the room. Other overly friendly ones will burst through the door, jump on me and lick my face. Challenger did none of these things; instead, she entered confident she would control this space, along with all things and creatures in it. In her short life, she had met no one she could not reign over and had no reason to believe I would be any different.

As I talked with her owners about the nightmare of living with this dog, Challenger proceeded to treat Theresa as if she were a favorite "chew toy," constantly grabbing her sweater and hands. For a few moments, the dog lay on the carpet and amused herself with pulling yarn from the carpet. I picked up the end of her leash and wiggled it to get her attention and stop the carpet chewing. Without hesitation, Challenger lunged at me, fully intending to bite me. Having the leash firmly in hand, I stopped the attack and told her "No"! Undaunted, as soon as her feet hit the floor, she lunged a second and third time. This four-month-old puppy's boldness surprised me. She had entered *my* territory and did not hesitate to issue a challenge. Her name suited her well. Only by standing up, towering over her sternly glaring, and commanding her in a deep growling voice I was able to stop the attacks.

Glad that I had witnessed Challenger in action, Harvey and Theresa proceeded to paint a very dismal picture of their experiences and explained how they had tried to cope with the dog so far. They had kept her in a crate most of the time, because they didn't know how else to control her. She was taken out for walks often but was not free to play in the house. Theresa felt such terrible guilt that she sometimes slept beside the crate, to be close to Challenger. Despite all the biting and bad behavior, Theresa passionately loved this puppy and would willingly do anything to help her.

I wasn't sure I could turn this puppy around because, at 16 weeks, she might be past the point of no return. She had bitten hard, countless times and that would remain in her memory. She had obviously not met anyone more powerful than herself. I agreed to try. The owners left her with me, for an attitude adjustment.

When I brought her into our kennel, and began to remove her collar, she tried to bite me again. I quickly took hold of both sides of her jowls, laid her on her back, stared into her eyes, and growled at her until she stopped struggling. I did not and would not hold her mouth closed. I strategically placed my hands in a way so that I would not get bitten. I do not agree with the advice that many people proclaim; to hold a biting puppy's mouth closed. Most often this will make a dominant puppy worse and may be too harsh for a sensitive puppy. I then proceeded to put the collar on and take it off several times, so that she would learn that I had the right to do that. Challenger never attempted to bite me again. She acknowledged my leadership.

Our first lesson accomplished, we continued with leadership and obedience training. She learned to, walk politely on a leash, wait at doors to allow me to go through them first, sit, stay, lie down, stay off furniture and people and allow me to handle her body. These were tremendous victories, but we still needed to address other behavior problems

As Challenger's behavior improved, I gave her more freedom, allowing her to run loose in the kennel area while I cleaned. Often, dogs like Challenger will steal things tissue from the wastebasket, remote controls, anything that will get the owners attention then become aggressive when a person attempts to retrieve them. It did not take long for her discover the joys of "surfing the kennels"! She would dash in, grab another dog's toy and retreat, hoping I would chase her and try to take the prize from her. I dealt with this, not by engaging in her game, but by teaching her to come when I blew a whistle. When she responded, I traded a treat and praise for the toy she had stolen. This worked well for the most part, until she escalated the contest, putting my control to the hardest test she could devise.

Still determined to get her way when she really wanted to keep a treasure she had stolen, one day she snatched a particularly flavorful, smoked bone. I could tell by her posturing that this would be different. Her body tensed. She knew our game, but didn't want to trade; she wanted both the bone and the treat. When I put my hand over her hovering, tense body, she growled at me. I knew I would have to respond instantly and firmly, as one dog would do to another in these circumstances; otherwise, the previous training would be lost. Because of our previous training and the respect she had for me, I was able to execute a stern verbal correction with dominant posturing and she allowed me to take the bone. I took it, gently petted her, and then gave it back, which might be surprising. To be sure she understood the point I was trying to make, I again petted her and gently took the bone. I again gave it back. By the third time I took the bone, she was relaxed and wagging her tail, anticipating that it would be shortly returned to her. Then I put her in the kennel with the bone so she could chew and enjoy it in peace. I bought several such bones and placed them around the kennel so that she could have them at will. I had worked through our toughest situation. She now allowed me to take away a stolen bone without any tension at all. She understood that the rules did not change. I removed the excitement of the fight and the need to be possessive. I did not fight with her, nor did I retreat or keep the bone. Yet I still remained the dominant one in control. <u>This should only be attempted by an experience professional trainer/behaviorist.</u> Often, the first time a dog growls or snaps, it is so surprising to the owner that they back away, allowing a dog to take a huge step up in the pecking order. Once a dog has gotten away with possessive aggression, it remembers and is well on its way to ruling the owners. If an inexperienced owner were to challenge their dog at this point it could be very dangerous.

The first time Challenger saw my grandchildren she tried to attack them through the fence. Using food treats, obedience, leadership and engaging my grandchildren, I changed her attitude toward children.

I felt the time had come, to re-introduce the dog to her owners. Although Challenger had made great steps and had not attempted to put her mouth on me or anyone else in my family, the minute she saw Theresa, the dog opened her mouth and prepared to resume her old tactics. After several training sessions with Theresa and Challenger, it was time to send them home to try it on their own. Although Theresa worked hard to be the leader she did not have a dominant nature and although she made a valiant effort, Challenger saw through the facade.

One Sunday morning, a few days later, I received a tearful call from Theresa. She and Challenger had had a battle of wills and Theresa had lost. The dog had bitten her again. This lady loved Challenger so much that she would part with her if it would save Challengers life. I agreed to take her and work with her until I felt comfortable placing her in a home with experienced handlers.

Challenger lived with my family, my husband, three children, a son-in-law, two grandchildren, six dogs, and me for six months. In that situation, the dog was obedient without aggression. She still persisted in stealing things, but showed no aggression when we traded for them. She spent a lot of time with my nine-year-old grandson, Alex, who wanted a dog that he could show in 4-H competitions. We allowed Alex to try that, but wanted to see if he would be responsible enough to own her, and most importantly, to see if Challenger would maintain a safe respect for him.

Challenger did maintain a safe respect for Alex to the point of now thinking she needed to protect him. She had given up the stealing and possessing, was very safe and tolerant with her own family, but was becoming untrustworthy around strangers. She was unpredictable, some strangers she took an instant liking to. Usually, she was happy, friendly and loving to everyone. Occasionally, she would lunge and snap at a stranger that moved to quickly around her family, especially Alex. The older she got the more frequent this happened. She had hit three years old, which is a common age for dogs to change and start looking at life through adult eyes with responsibilities and letting loose of puppy ways. She had not bitten anyone since she left her first owners, but we could see the signs and it was coming. This dog had suppressed her aggressive tendencies for a while, but with the escalation of her lunging, growling and snapping at strangers we knew it was only a matter of time before the biting began again. Ours is a very social family with children coming and going often. Only because of all the training, socializing, dog experience and our family being diligent about following proper leadership steps was she safe to live with as long as she had been. If one of Alex's friends moved to fast around him she would quickly without any warning jump at the child with a vicious snap. Minutes before she would have been very friendly with that same child. Seriously considering all our options, we had to do the responsible thing. Challenger was becoming more dangerous and euthanasia was the sensible choice.

*Challenger was the exception. She had extreme aggression with little chance of mending it. The following story shows a dog that was not by nature aggressive, the problem was easily reparable because it was caught early enough and proper steps were followed.*

### "Cliff"

I tried to console the sobbing lady on the phone. The owner of the six-month-old Golden Retriever cried hysterically, saying that her dog was aggressive and would have to be put to sleep. I had talked to Molly Brown several times before she purchased the fluffy, blond puppy and had even done a private lesson with her when she brought the puppy home. She had previously owned a Golden Retriever that had displayed what is commonly called "Rage Syndrome," a serious aggression problem that erupts with little apparent motivation and rarely improves or disappears, even with training. The simple act of retrieving something the dog has stolen or even moving the dog from its resting place can prompt vicious attacks. Her previous dog had to be euthanized, and Molly feared she faced the same situation.

Molly had gone to great lengths to make a good choice. She had visited the puppy daily, before bringing it home. She had called me several times for advice about her choice. She had brought the puppy to me for an evaluation. While this adorable little dog was slow to learn commands, he seemed gentle and cuddly and showed no signs of aggressive tendencies. I suspected that Molly, in her fear of reliving her previous experience, had somehow prompted the aggression she was now seeing; but I didn't want to rush to judgment until I could see the dog and know more. This frantic call came only four months after I had sent her home with instructions about raising the dog. I needed to see the dog and evaluate the situation.

    Molly arrived with Cliff, his food and dish. I hardly recognized the dog as the roly-poly puppy I had seen four months ago. Leggy, tall, and very thin, I could see his ribs through his long, blond Golden Retriever coat. Clearly, something had gone badly wrong.

    I needed answers to many questions such as when the aggressive behavior had begun, how it had escalated, and how Molly had responded. What came out was that she had tried to manipulate his food in order to establish her own leadership and in doing so, had threatened his food supply, causing him to react with hostility. In the midst of Cliff's eating she would remove his food, to show him she had the right to do that. When he protested with a low growl, she not only kept the food, she yelled at him and pushed him into his crate. The next day she tried it again. Each day, he growled sooner and with more ferocity, growing hungrier and more impatient. The problem continued to worsen until thankfully she called me. Molly was by no means a cruel person. She truly thought she was training her new puppy to be safe with his food.

    I asked her to demonstrate the obedience and tricks Cliff had learned. Indeed, he performed impressively. He would sit, lie down, come, shake, roll over, and perform various tricks on command. Obviously, he had responded well to his training. This only confirmed my original suspicions that she had created the food-aggression problem.

More questions, answers, and experimentation moved us along a road to correcting the behavior. Molly explained that she could feed him treats by hand and used them in training without a problem. As I soaked dry kibble in water and prepared to feed Cliff, Molly squirmed in her seat, concerned about the amount of food I put into the bowl. I learned that she had been feeding him only two cups of dog food, per day. A growing Golden Retriever puppy can easily consumed twice that amount without gaining excessive weight. This poor puppy never had the luxury of feeling full. If he growled, Molly withdrew even the small amount he did receive.

Once Cliff's kibble was well soaked, I began feeding him by hand. As he gently removed the food from my hand, Molly became more anxious, worrying that I would overfeed him, although I only fed him about two cups. I explained that the soaking expands his food, giving the dog a sense of fullness without overfeeding calories. The happy dog could not believe that I continued to offer him food. I watched carefully for any sign that he might be feeling satisfied. As soon as he looked away from the food and me, I took that as a sign that he had eaten his fill and quit feeding him.

I sent Molly home with instructions designed to help them make a transition to the desired behaviors. She was to soak three cups of kibble and feed Cliff by hand, as I had done. Because the dog had grown so thin, I told her give him an additional small bowl of food each day if he seemed hungry. After two weeks, she was to set the dish on the floor and put a small portion of his meal into it. When the dish was empty and Cliff looked at her for more she would pick up the dish and add another handful of food. Repeating this over a period of a couple of weeks would teach Cliff that when Molly reached for his dish, she would be adding food, not taking it away. When this step was going well, she should put half of the food into the dish, let him finish that amount, pick it up, and then put the remainder into the dish. To underscore the behavior and establish a pleasant association with eating, she needed to say Cliff's name cheerfully while he ate and drop a special treat into his dish. I felt confident that following these instructions would solve the problem.

A call from Molly, a few weeks later, confirmed my initial evaluation. The problem had been created by Molly and changing her approach to feeding altered the behavior. The aggression had totally disappeared. She thanked me wholeheartedly, for saving her dog's life. This time with tears of joy.

### *Does your dog show aggression when there is pain involved?*

Pain is a natural way that animals learn. It is important to a dog's survival. If a porcupine hurts it, it learns quickly not to play with porcupines. If you do something that is uncomfortable to your dog it will naturally try to avoid the discomfort again. If your dog does not have a proper respect and trust, it may snap, growl or bite when you pull on a mat, have to clean a sore ear or cut its toenails. The importance of your dog trusting you are often demonstrated when it's time for grooming or veterinary care. If a dog snaps when it is hurting and the discomfort stops it seems logical to the dog to continue that behavior. If I could get away with it, I may try it myself when the dentist has his hands poking around in my mouth. But I know that would not be for my best interest and your dog should also understand that it is not for its best interest to snap at you. Even if your dog hates having its toenails cut that should not be an excuse to snap. It doesn't hurt to have the toenails cut (assuming you don't cut the qwik), but the dog fears that it will hurt and doesn't want to take any chances. The more the dog resists, the higher the chances it will get injured. Resulting with a dog that was sure it was going to hurt and does.

Cutting toenails and grooming are often the nightmare of dogs and owners. Dogs know the dreaded clippers. The more they protest, the worse the battle, the firmer it becomes ingrained into their "I will never let you cut my toenails again" category. You can try to correct this by gently massaging your dog, especially the feet, until the dog is relaxed and comfortable. Then try clipping or brushing, but most dogs know the difference and when the clippers or comb come out they escape as fast at they can. Training and respect is your best chance. "You may not like this doggie, but you must stay still because I said so." Tying your dog down and sitting on it is not the recommended technique. It may be best to take your dog for professional grooming and toenails on a regular basis. Please don't wait until your dog is matted to the skin and the toenails are so long that they are beginning to curl under. This will cause your dog to hate grooming and handling even more. It won't do much for your relationship with your groomer, either.

Perceived pain is a common problem, but can be difficult to diagnose. Perceived pain means "beware"! This has hurt before and might hurt again". It was hurt in the past so the dog is very guarded to prevent any pain from happening again. It can be difficult to know if the dog actually hurts or just thinks it is going to be hurt. To help you determine this I often recommend an experienced dog massage therapist. A skilled professional can often get to the bottom of the problem. They can also show you how to get your dog to relax and enjoy the touching.

We don't always know why a dog is hurting. It may have been running hard at the park and twisted its leg or back, but you were unaware of the incident. You then proceed to call it into the car to go home. It doesn't hop right in so you help out by lifting your dog into the car. Normally not a problem, this time it hurts when you pick it up. The next time you go to the park your dog may be resistant to coming close to the car or may be worried about you picking it up. Your dog may not hurt anymore, but you now have a problem that was caused by pain. Your first step is to determine for sure that your dog is not in pain by checking with a veterinarian and/or animal massage therapist. Once you have determined that your dog's problem behavior is caused by *perceived* pain rather than *actual* pain, you can take these steps to desensitize it. To work through the previous example of the dog injuring itself at the park you would gently pick your dog up in your house, when it doesn't relate being picked up to the park or car. Do this several times a day. Reward it with treats and praise. Once your dog relaxes when you pick it up in the house, go to the car and pick it up and put it in the car. Once your dog is in the car reward with treats and praise. Try this is in different locations. After your dog is totally relaxed with the previous step you would try it at the park where the injury happened. The point is to slowly desensitize the problem and convince your dog that it will no longer hurt. Do this only after you are sure the dog really doesn't have any more pain.

To desensitize a dog from a perceived pain problem think about how you can break it down into small steps. Once the dog is comfortable with each step then you can start putting the steps together.
Sometimes the pain has happened too many times and it is firmly ingrained in the dog's memory. There is no way you will convince the dog to trust that it won't hurt. Sometimes the pain happened during the age of fear imprint, which means the time in the dog's life when something scary happens and the dog will never forget. The age for this is usually between eight and eleven weeks and again somewhere between seven and twelve months.

Each dog has a different pain tolerance. I have seen some dogs that scream if you look too hard at them and others that don't wince if they get stepped on by a horse. Some dogs are more emotionally sensitive to pain and feel betrayed if they experience any discomfort. Some dogs have memories that will last until death and others totally forget about it as soon as the next thought enters their brain. If the dog truly has to endure something that is going to be painful, such as cleaning out an infected ear, it is crucial that your dog respects you enough to know it has to allow it. If you do not trust your dog to tolerate your handling its sore ear, don't take chances, use a muzzle. Once a dog bites and learns that biting is an option, then you have began a whole new problem.

*The following true story shows a dog that was unfairly treated in its past and perceived pain was a big issue. It was unable to live in a home without serious desensitizing and obedience training.*

### "Choco": No Touching Allowed

"Please, please help us," began the familiar plea of the desperate dog lover sitting in the rescue shelter. "The examining vet advised us to put her to sleep, but she doesn't deserve that; she's aggressive, but it's not her fault." The vet had not been able to do a thorough examination, because Choco had fought and bitten hysterically when he tried to touch her. The young women students of the Vet Tec school had rescued Choco and having no other choice, had been keeping the dog in their car until they could find another home. They were living in an apartment that did not permit dogs. Remarkably, Choco behaved well in the car, a clue that she was not innately destructive. The abuse she had suffered in her previous home had conditioned her to have violent reactions when handled.

    Abuse takes many forms: physical violence, neglect, abandonment, deprivation, and even indifference. Most people understand the difference between abuse and discipline, some do not. Others know the difference, but ignore it when driven by personal pressures or when conflicts between the owner's personality and the dog's arise. Those do occur.

    Dogs, like humans, react to abuse in various ways. Some cower and withdraw, suffering silently in any escape corner they can find, preferring no attention to the kind they have learned to expect. Others have such a strong sense of survival and self that they fight back, returning abuse for abuse, often against formidable odds. Choco fought back and established barriers he would not permit people to cross without protests and consequences.

    Choco's former situation was anything but warm and fuzzy. The violent husband battered his wife, children and dog. Choco even had a stiff, permanently damaged leg, because the man had kicked her across the room. The parents would leave the children and the dog home alone for days at a time. No one, parents or children, even bothered to take the dog outside. Not a house I would want to visit without a gas mask. Choco needed boarding care and training, which costs money the students did not have.

Shelters have extremely limited resources, often having nothing to choose from, but bad alternatives. Investing in boarding and training, with no guarantees that we could rehabilitate the dog and find her a home was not an option. As I pondered the situation, I couldn't help notice Choco's response as one of the women gently stroked the dog's head. Choco laid her head on the girl's leg, obviously grateful for the tender touch. She did appear to want more comforting touch.

Fortunately, Choco had arrived at an opportune time. I was training a young woman, Mary, to be a canine behaviorist. She had ample experience training dogs in routine manners, but lacked skills in solving complicated behavior problems. We carefully studied Choco's appealing, 65-pound body, covered with a clean, short, sable coat. Although she limped on her damaged leg she was quite active as she moved awkwardly around the room. "Do we want to take this one on?" I asked my student. Mary responded immediately and enthusiastically, eager for the experience. Choco came home with me and our three month adventure with Choco at my house began.

When an animal has trusted and had that trust shattered, it will never completely let its guard down again. If the animal lives through nature's hard lessons, it will become wary and not repeat mistakes. Choco had learned her survival lessons well. She would never again tolerate what she considered hostile touching without reacting aggressively, although her birth temperament seemed sound and not prone to aggression. When someone touched her in a way she didn't understand, she reacted quickly, baring her teeth and snapping. If I so much as took hold of her collar, moved her, or touched her near her injured leg, she "cautioned" me with a show of sharp teeth. If I did not heed her warnings, she followed with a vicious snap or swift bite. She presented a major challenge. Her saving grace was that when she did bite, she applied very little pressure and did not actually injure anyone. If she had bitten hard I could not consider placing her in a home.

After careful assessment, we set training goals. Choco would:

1. Allow people to touch her body, comfortably, including her bad leg, without displaying aggression.

2. Learn basic obedience commands: sit, stay, come, and down.

3. Learn tricks and retrieving, enjoy her training and being with people.

4. Walk on a leash without pulling.

5. Enter a dog crate and accept spending time in it.

6. Permit her cherished bone to be taken away without hostile reactions.

She had already experienced the ultimate unfair correction, abuse; therefore, physical correction for improper behavior would only escalate her aggression problem and reinforce her fears. We began much as a foster parent might with a child from an abusive situation. We did not baby her spoil her, or allow her to control us, we provided structure and guidance fairly. She needed good, caring leaders she could trust and that's what she got.

Favorite treats work wonders with dogs like Choco, especially when combined with lots of affection and praise. I cannot emphasize this enough, when dealing with a dog that has suffered abuse. We mastered sitting before she received a treat fairly quickly. From that stage, we moved to sitting and allowing her body to be touched. Being very cautious, we touched her head and slowly inched down her neck and spine. Any quick move would trigger an aggressive snap. We did light, gentle massage until she relaxed, allowing us to work down her legs. At any point, if she seemed uncomfortable, we reversed the direction, returning to her comfort zone. A display of teeth sent a clear message she was getting uncomfortable. "Retreating" did not amount to allowing Choco to control us or the situation, rather it allayed her fears and reinforced her trust. It may appear as though we were letting her have her way, but working with a dog like Choco, who had suffered severe abuse, requires a different approach from that used with dogs that dominated their environment and owners have spoiled them allowing that control. We did not want her to see any similarities between her former owners and us. After about eight weeks, she allowed us to handle her entire body, including her injured leg. Each positive response netted a treat, more affection and praise.

She rewarded our patience, eventually responding to all basic commands and happily joining my own pack of dogs in searching and retrieving games around the pasture. Although the injured leg remained stiff, it did not seem to cause her pain. She had learned to trust us to touch and examine her and cut her toenails. She would even crawl into our laps, inviting more affection and would relinquish a cherished bone. Inducing her to "share" her bone required the same patience the other steps had required. Respecting her comfort zone was a key factor. After several sessions, she allowed us to take the bone, but it was important that we always gave it back. Choco did fine as long as she had a routine she could count on. Changes in her routine brought panic reactions and attempts to bite, but the bites did not cause us pain. The improvement was fantastic.

These gains did not come easily quickly or without threats to us. At times in the early training stages, three people helped using several restraints, including a "halti," a device that fits over a dogs head much like a halter for a horse. This prevented her from swinging her head and biting us. This was to insure everyone's safety, At no time, did we use the equipment for corrections.

We moved on to our next challenge, finding a single person living a routine life and willing to adopt a special-needs dog with aggression problems and a bum leg.

Although, the women who had brought the dog to us searched relentlessly, they found no takers. I, personally, might have given up. Begging the local animal shelter got results. The shelter agreed to take Choco and find her a suitable home. Although Choco had adjusted to Mary, my family and me, I had reservations about her ability to transfer to the multiple strangers at the shelter. It was thrilling to see that when the manager hugged her, she permitted him to examine her leg, something she would never have allowed when we began her training. Yes, the training would transfer to strangers, I was relieved. Choco was left with written instructions on what was the best type of home for her and the proper way to handle her.

**The search for a new home did not take long. Choco now lives with a person who understands and cherishes her. Training dogs can certainly be a rewarding career.**

# Chapter 3

## *Does your dog show any aggression toward strangers?*

There are various reasons why many dogs are not comfortable with strangers. It is their nature to be territorial and cautious of intruders. Depending on their placement in their pack structure, they may also be protective, possessive or fearful. It is not always easy to determine which reason is causing your dog's aggression problem, but finding the cause will aid you in correcting the behavior.

*Does your dog growl, bark, snap or bite strangers?*

The following is a break down of the different categories of aggression toward strangers:

- *Is your dog only aggressive when in its own territory?*
- *Is your dog aggressive only when behind a barrier?*
- *Is your dog protective of the owner?*
- *Is your dog fearful?*
- *Is your dog only aggressive toward men or children?*
- *Has your dog recently had puppies, been in season, or been bred?*
- *Do the parents or littermates have any aggression problems?*

**Is your dog only aggressive when in its own territory?**

Canines naturally have an urge to guard their territory, especially if they are of a dominant or fearful nature. Some dogs are so confident and love everyone so much, that they wouldn't give a thought to keeping people away. Others suddenly become brave and aggressive only when they are safely restrained behind a barrier. Your dog's territory may include your yard, neighborhood, car, crate, kennel or a ten-foot circle around you.

If your dog barks to alert you that someone has arrived and once you are there to take over, your dog settles down, that it quite normal and not what I consider an aggression problem. Dogs that charge people in a very confrontational manner are getting more serious. Be especially concerned if the dog rises on its hind legs getting upright and closer to the intruders face while barking. Sometimes it will take the experience of a professional dog trainer to be able to read whether the dog just has very bad manners or is truly acting aggressive. Putting its mouth on the visitor in any manner is to be taken very seriously.

In the case of a dominant, territorial dog, solid obedience training and excellent leadership is critical in controlling this problem. This type of dog must understand that it is *your* territory and not *their* job to protect it. Have your dog on leash and teach it to approach people and sit politely. It is not required or even recommended that the visitors pet your dog. Do not allow your dog to get any closer to the visitor than you are comfortable, keeping it under safe control. You may be able to convince your dog that it cannot chase away visitors when you are there to take control of the situation, but if you are not there, do not trust it to use dependable judgment on its own. Do not set your dominant territorial dog up for trouble; make sure it is well confined, ideally in a location that it cannot see if anyone is entering its territory.

Fearful dogs can appear to be quite dominant and aggressive, but are only acting that way because they are truly afraid. Building confidence is the best way to help this situation. If you are not sure if your dog is dominant or fearful you can still try the following steps to see if the behavior improves.

**You build confidence by following the steps below:**
- Be a good leader. If it is clear that you are handling the situation, your dog can relax and allow you to deal with the intruder.

- Teach your dog how you *want* it to act. Many people are good at correcting the dog for unwanted behavior, but never really teach the dog what they want it to do. If you are very clear and consistent with what behavior you want, most dogs will greatly improve. This may seem simple, but most people get distracted and forget to reward the desirable behavior. When company arrives take this opportunity to have a training session. Have a leash on your dog before you open the door, correct unwanted behavior and be sure to reward good behavior.
- Use obedience to teach your dog to sit, lay down or go to its bed. This helps make it very clear to the dog that it does not have to worry and if it listens to you all will be okay. You are in control of the situation.

If your dog has already bitten, ripped clothing, or snapped at an intruder entering into its territory, you must take great caution. Prevention is your safest strategy. Use a combination of obedience backed up with a physical restraint. For example, if your dog might bite a person coming into your house, before you let them in, send your dog away from the door to its bed. As a safety precaution tie it to something solid so it physically cannot get to your visitor. You may have to go so far as to put your dog outside or secure it in another room before letting company into your house. Know your dog and don't take chances with peoples safety. **Never** open your door with one hand and hold onto your dog's collar with the other when you are greeting visitors. This action will cause your dog to become very protective and aggressive. Make sure your dog is secured away from the door before you open it.

A dog learns quickly, if it goes running and barking at people that are going by, those people leave. The dog doesn't know that those people were going to leave anyway. It starts forming a very bad habit of chasing people away, which can become quite serious. Sometimes the people going by aggravate the problem by teasing the dog. Never tie a dog in a situation where it can see people going by. Restricting your dog's ability to escape from an uncomfortable situation can cause an aggressive, territorial reaction. If your dog is territorial about your yard, you should have it in an area where it doesn't see people going by. A smaller fenced area behind your house often works well.

To correct this bad habit, take your dog into the problem situation with a leash on and practice its obedience exercises. Insist that your dog sits or lays down while people pass by. Do not allow growling or barking. Keep your dog's attention on you. Make sure you follow all the leadership steps also. It may take weeks or even months to convince the dog to relax and not be concerned about the strangers. Accomplishment does not mean that your dog should now be left alone in the yard because the territorial problem can return very quickly.

### *Is your dog aggressive only when behind a barrier?*

A common reaction for a dog that is in its car, crate or kennel is to act violent to scare an intruder away. Often they have no intention of biting; they just feel very intimidated and want to be left alone. One reason they act aggressively is that they feel trapped and know they can't get away. Another reason is that they have the right to be left alone by strangers when they are in their den, bed or special place. I have seen some of the most gentle dogs act very aggressively when they are confined, but they never act this way any other time. They learn quickly that a sudden burst of noise and teeth will effectively back away almost any intruder. Although it startles strangers and embarrasses owners, this type of aggression usually is not worth worrying over. Do take caution if this is not the only time you see aggression from this dog.

*The following true story shows the ultimate of barrier aggression. This dog also had aggression at other times and the only thing that saved her was that she only weighed about six pounds.*

### **Sassy: My Car, My Kingdom!**

Having spent much of my day working with somber problems, I found Mr. Jones to be refreshing and enjoyable to work with. He entered the evaluation room with a congenial smile on his face and a delicate, attractive Pomeranian resting comfortably in his arms.

"Hi, I hope you can help me with Sassy," he laughed, then seated himself on the sofa and placed the miniature menace on the floor. "Actually, I don't think Sassy is as big a problem as my family. They won't let anyone correct her. She is so spoiled. She sleeps in my granddaughter's bed and when I go to tuck the child in at night, this little brat growls at me. If I tell her "No," my wife and daughter think I am terrible. Is it so bad to correct such a small dog?" he asked.

Of course it isn't. Size has nothing to do with the need for discipline and training. Pomeranians as a breed can be a challenge, particularly if the owners pamper them excessively. We tend to indulge tiny creatures, especially ones as fluffy and winsome as Pomeranians.

As Mr. Jones continued to describe Sassy's behaviors, I observed her as she walked around the room, investigating everything, behaving perfectly normally. When she came close to me, I picked her up and set her in my lap where she sat contentedly, showing no signs of aggression, dominance or shyness. I honestly wondered if he were talking about the dog in my lap or another one.

He continued to explain that the dog ran their house, getting anything she desired and doing what she wanted. Anyone who interfered got a painful bite as a reminder. "I would be happy if we could just fix this car thing that she does," he stated. He tried to explain how she reacted in the car, I just had to see it for myself. As we headed outside to his car I began to hand Sassy to him, but he was not willing to take her from me. "Oh no," he laughed, "you must put her down, then I can pick her up without getting bitten!" I obligingly put Sassy on the floor so that he could safely pick her up. Sassy did not like being taken out of anyones arms, even if it was her owner taking her from a stranger. We headed for the car.

    I will never forget the events that followed. Mr. Jones placed Sassy in the passenger seat, climbed in and started the car. He then shut off the engine and turned his back on the deceivingly cute little dog to exit the vehicle. She briskly ran straight up his back, barking viciously at him as though she was the newest type of car-jacking. He quickly hopped out and shut the door. We watched through the window as she continued to bark hysterically, showing her teeth and covering the driver's side window with slimy saliva. She was daring anyone to touch the car she had just stolen from Mr. Jones. It was just about the funniest sight I had ever seen. Granted, if this were a sixty pound dog instead of a six pound dog, no one would be laughing. But to see something that cute and small put so much effort into looking vicious was comical. Naturally, I wondered what happened when he tried to re-enter the car. He proceeded to demonstrate. He carefully opened the door, just enough that he could grasp an empty cardboard paper towel roll he kept in the space between the seat and door. Armed with the roll, he beat her back until this mini-tyrant retreated to the passenger seat. Once he was in position to drive, Sassy stopped all aggression and relaxed for the anticipated drive. It was truly hilarious, but only because she was so small and couldn't inflict serious injury to the man.

    "What can I do about this?" Mr. Jones asked. I suggested that he put a leash on Sassy and attach it to the passenger door before he exited the car so that she couldn't get into his seat at all. I also reassured him that he didn't have to put up with that kind of behavior. He should then continue getting in and out of the car until she sat quietly with no aggression at all. He could not believe that correcting this annoying problem was as simple as to just tie her up to the passenger doorknob. It was his reaction to that small, simple suggestion that gave me insight into the depth of the problem at home. I encouraged him to get further training for Sassy and told him to get her out of his granddaughter's bed, letting him know that I would be available if he or any of his family wanted help training her. He explained that there wasn't a chance of changing the dog's sleeping arrangement, when no one in the family would even tell her "No". He thanked me explaining that he just wanted reassurance that correcting the dog was okay and went blissfully on his way. I have not heard from him since, but the vision of Sassy, the little monster in the car, will stay forever in my memory.

### *Is your dog protective?*

Protective or possessive? Maybe the same action, but for very different reasons. People like to think their dogs are loyal and would protect them if necessary. Some dogs will; some dogs won't. I have found that if your dog growls when someone approaches you, it is most likely that the dog thinks it owns you and doesn't want to share rather than it is protecting you. For a dog to protect you, it must feel you are in danger. Many times when a dog shows aggression when someone approaches its owner, the dog knows that their owner is not in danger. Instead your dog is saying, "Back off! She belongs to me".

Of course, there are cases where a dog does believe the owner and/or itself are in danger and will show some aggression at that point. We hope that the dog will put on a good front, but not follow through with biting. It is best if dogs don't know they can bite.

If your dog does act aggressively when a stranger approaches you, the further you are from your dog the less possessive it will act. You may have to tie it across the room or a distance away, so your dog can see that you are okay and handling the situation. You need to give your dog the message that its not its job to keep people away from you. The closer a dog is to its owner, the more often the protective or possessive aggression will occur. If your dog has good obedience training, you can command it to go away from you, lie down and stay. Using obedience commands makes it very clear to the dog who is in charge and what its job is.

Some breeds are genetically prone to being very protective. If you own a naturally protective breed, you will want to make sure your dog has excellent obedience and be diligent in preventing an accident from happening.

*If you have ever doubted the importance of how genetics affects behavior, the protective breed in the following true story may convince you.*

## "Brute": One-Man Dog and Jaguar Hunter

"The Fila Mastiff is the world's finest, natural estate guardian and family protection dog. It hunts Jaguar and needs no training to protect." Quote taken from a Fila Mastiff web site.

All Filas are not as protective and aggressive as Brute, but most do have a strong protective nature.

People searching for a family pet need to understand some of the special vocabulary some breeders may use to describe their breed. The word "independent" often translates to mean the breed is stubborn, strong –willed, and refuses to come when it is called. "Active" may mean that the dog bounces off sofas and needs constant attention. The phrase "naturally protective" should raise questions and cause concern. In this case the phrase indicates that the dog hunts Jaguars. Few people in this country have a need for a Jaguar hunter since the big cat is native to tropical areas of South America. People owning a hundred-square-mile plantation in a remote area might conceivably need a patrol dog with the temperament and traits of a Fila, but they should consider the seriousness of living in suburbia with neighborhood children visiting. The "world's finest natural estate guardian" would hardly be an appropriate choice.

## When Friendly Dogs Bite

George and Lydia Johnson purchased a Fila and embarked on the experience quite unprepared. Although the breeder had given frank warnings, the couple associated Filas with Rottweilers, Doberman Pinschers and German Shepherds, all of which they had previously owned. Filas are not the same kind of animal.

The puppy they brought to my home was, without a doubt, the most dangerous dog I have ever been asked to evaluate. When they called for help, I considered declining, but agreed. After all at 20 weeks, how bad could it be? When they pulled into the driveway, I went to greet them. George told me to go ahead, that he would bring the dog after Emily and I were in the evaluation room. I found this odd, but complied thinking the man might not have the puppy on a leash. He explained that he did have it on a leash, but feared the dog, who was already growling and baring his teeth, would break loose and bite me.

Emily and I settled in the evaluation room watching as the 80 lb., brindle-colored "puppy" planted his giant feet and hauled his owner through the door. I prayed that the leash would hold having no doubt that Brute would love to get a hold of me, a stranger. I sat still and nonthreatening. Once everyone was seated, I watched the dog study me, glaring straight into my eyes, never flinching or diverting his stare—a bold act for a puppy entering my territory. As long as I didn't move, he remained quiet; if I as much as moved my hand, he lunged toward me ferociously barking and snarling, often catching George off guard and coming much closer than I would have liked.

I could understand why the couple had found Brute attractive. He was a gorgeous animal with beautiful tiger striping and overwhelmingly large feet. I did ask if they had accurately reported his age given his weight. They assured me it was correct. This dog would easily grow to 180 lbs. Brute had qualities other than beauty. Friendly and gentle with his owners, a Fila trait, he happily and promptly responded to the obedience commands as George demonstrated what the dog had learned. Brute heeled properly, sat and lay down when told; none of these things would make this animal safe with strangers if George did not have a good hold of the leash. George had not seen this as a problem since he and his wife had few visitors. One, however, could be one too many. I needed many answers before I could make recommendations: why they had chosen this breed, how had they accommodated Brute at their home and what adjustments did they plan to make.

    Essentially, they had sought a protector for Emily because George worked nights. They got a protector all right, but they also had a dog with killer instincts. Again, I plied them with questions about the information the breeder had given them. The breeder, they reported, had bluntly explained the seriousness of owning a Fila, but they had not understood until they began to experience first hand the power and temperament of this dog. Emily went on to describe what they saw when they approached the breeder's property—a fort surrounded by triple, eight-foot fences. "Didn't that give you a clue?" I wondered, but didn't ask. I asked if they had installed similar barriers on their property, but they did not have even one fence, just a kennel several yards from the house.

    I asked them to describe the security measures they had taken. Part of their property was surrounded with horse fencing. That keeps most horses in, but dogs, even large ones, can go through and under it with little problem. Essentially, they had no effective barriers against either Brute's escape or people entering. Emily went on explaining that Brute stayed in a kennel during the day and she brought him into the house at night. This was fine except they had no fencing between the kennel and the house. A Fila can never be off leash unless secured behind a sturdy, high fence. Any sudden distraction could send Brute flying to investigate or worse.

The couple had considered taking steps to socialize Brute, but those steps placed others and themselves at risk. They had thought about taking Brute on leash into town hoping he would get used to strangers and accept them. While early socializing can sometimes help, accommodating strangers goes against the basic nature of the animal. Taking Brute into a situation like that would be tantamount to walking into a town with a bomb at the end of the leash.

Emily asked if she could try working with Brute to see if he would obey her as well as he had obeyed her husband. George nervously handed her the leash, cautioning her to hold it tightly and not release it. Brute walked with Emily politely and sat when asked to do so. This pleased Emily so much that she dropped the leash to give the dog a hug. I froze in my chair not even daring to breathe, as George leaped out of his and grabbed the leash, ordering Emily never to do that again. Only minutes had passed before she repeated the mistake. This time, George and I both had enough of Emily working with Brute. George took Brute back to sit with him. I had seen enough to know that it was only a matter of time before the dog seriously injured or killed someone.

The time had come to explain options and measures the couple would have to consider if they chose to keep this dog. For starters, they would have to install secure fencing. The dog would have to wear a basket style muzzle all the time. The basket muzzles allow the dog to bark, pant and drink. He could still injure a person by knocking them down, but probably couldn't kill someone. I saved my strongest recommendation for last—return the dog to the breeder.

As a trainer, I feel tremendous responsibility for people's safety. The advice I give can affect some unknowing stranger's life. I was glad I had the opportunity to talk with George and Emily before a tragedy occurred rather than meet them in court after someone had been hurt.

Those were not bad people; they just walked into a situation beyond their abilities. Brute was not a bad Fila, he was beautiful and a prime example of the breed, behaviorally and in every other way. These owners and that dog made a dangerous combination. The Johnson's left planning to return the dog to the breeder.

### *Is your dog fearful?*

Reading a dog's body language is not always as straightforward as you might think. Sometimes it is quite obvious that a dog is reacting fearfully and other times the dog appears to be very bold and dominant, but behind the public display the dog is utterly afraid.

***Typical fear based posturing may show some or all of the following*:**

- **Ears back**
- **Tail low or between rear legs**

- **Body low and leaning slightly back**
- **Eyes open wide and often with whites showing**
- **Hair raised on back**
- **Lips quivering or baring teeth**

You must look at the entire picture your dog is showing. Just because your dog lays its ears back and lowers its tail when someone reaches to pet it, does not always mean that it is afraid. It may be showing respect for the person approaching, not wanting to challenge in anyway. Hackles up on the back may mean the dog is excited or a little nervous.

Baring of teeth, rising of hackles, growling and backing away from the person approaching are definitely signs of fear. Some dogs, no matter how afraid, would not consider biting, but many find that the best way to get the stranger to leave them alone is to growl, snap or bite. These dogs learn quickly that the hostile approach works; therefore, they refine this technique and become more offensive with their aggression. This makes the dog appear very dominant, rather than fearful. If you follow the instructions for correcting the fearful aggression problem and the dog improves, you can assume that the aggression was due to fear.

Fear aggression is usually correctable _if_ the behavior has not become too ingrained. Steps for correcting fearful aggression all involve building the dog's confidence.

*The following steps will help you build your dogs confidence around strangers:*

- Become a good leader for your dog. Your dog must believe that you will take care of it and that it does not need to be afraid. By following the leadership steps described previously in this book, your dog will learn to trust you to protect and care for him/her.

- Use a tasty treat. If the stranger is willing, have him/her drop an appetizing treat close to your dog. Notice I said drop, <u>not</u> reach out and expect the scared dog to take the treat from the hand. There are several reasons I say this: The dog may not notice the treat and may think the person is reaching out to pet or grab it. Also, if the person is afraid or tense, the dog will notice and this may trigger the dog to snap. You may also become tense not knowing if the dog will snap. Your dog will be very aware of the tension and become more afraid. Simply dropping the treat on the ground removes all the tension. It also gives the dog a choice to take the treat or not. You will know the dog is getting more relaxed when it takes the treat.

- As the stranger drops a treat to the dog he/her should speak friendly and confidently. "Hi doggie. How are you doing? Do you want a cookie?"

- Use a soft basket style muzzle to help everyone relax. Get your dog used to wearing the muzzle before it is allowed to be around strangers. Do not feel sad, embarrassed or sorry for your dog when it wears the muzzle. Keep in mind that muzzling the dog is for everyone's best interest. Do not use the style of muzzle that holds the dogs mouth closed. Your dog should easily be able to pant. The muzzles that the greyhounds use are very comfortable for the dogs to wear. Unfortunately there are some breeds that the muzzles won't fit because of the shape of their face.

- Do not allow a stranger to pet the dog when it is afraid. If the dog is comfortable, allow it to go up and sniff the stranger. Of course, you must know your dog. If you cannot trust your dog not to bite, do not allow it to get too close. If you are not relaxed with the situation you can bet that your dog is not relaxed. Don't force it.

- Never force your dog to be pet by holding or restraining him/her. This can be very terrifying for fearful dogs and often leaves them no choice except to growl, snap or bite.

- If the stranger is in your house, you can tie your dog in the room so it can watch what is going on and get accustomed to the stranger from a distance. It is important for you to instruct your company to stay away from the dog. If your dog is relaxing your company may toss a treat to the dog.

- If you are away from your house, it is important to stay relaxed, breathe normally and do not tighten up on your dog's leash. Tightening the leash is equivalent to pulling the trigger, telling your dog that everyone is worried about the approaching stranger. You should talk pleasantly to your dog and offer it a special treat or toy to relax the situation, taking the focus off the stranger. Sometimes the act of touching the person's arm will show your dog that there is no need for concern.

- Teach your dog basic obedience so you can use it to let your dog know that if it does what you instruct, all is well. If you take control of a scary situation by commanding your dog to sit, lay down, stay or leave it will help your dog's confidence.

- Be very clear to your dog about what you want it to do. Many dogs are afraid because they don't know what they are supposed to do when a stranger approaches. Simply asking your dog to sit may help relax the situation. Use your previously trained obedience commands.

- Take control, stay calm and be clear on instructing your dog what to do.

- Using a friendly dog as a good role model can also be very helpful. Let the fearful dog watch as the confidant social dog gets petted and enjoys the attention.

*If any dog had the right to be a fear-biter it would be the dog in the following story, but fortunately this dog did not attempt any aggression.*

### Cleo: Return from the Wild

only a litter of puppies delivered under a shed on the discovering family's property.

The family that finally trapped her had struggled for eleven months to accomplish the challenge. When the puppies could leave their mother, the people crawled under the shed and removed the entire litter. They took them to the shelter, which placed them into appropriate homes, but they couldn't capture Cleo immediately. Finally, because she stayed close to the shed hoping to find her babies, the family succeeded. They had to carry her since she had no experience with a leash. Normally, carrying a feral dog would poExcited, as always, for a new and different experience with troubled dogs, I headed for the animal shelter to meet one of their new charges—a feral dog we named "Cleo". When I arrived, they introduced me to a forty pound, brindle-colored female that appeared to be a Chinese Sharpei-Pit Bull mix. Cleo became another class project. The possibility of aggression concerned me, but not my inexperienced, fearless students.

A feral dog's background combines so many unknown factors, that assessing and working with them can be a challenge. We can only guess the breed mix, which may include not only domestic breeds, but also coyotes. While traits in purebred animals vary, they produce more predictable behaviors. The added unknowns about the dog's environment and socialization make for a complex and often perplexing creature. If a pack raised the animal, be it an animal or human pack, the pack will have conditioned it and prepared it to survive in that situation. If the dog, grew up as a loner, it will behave differently. With the number of abandoned animals and the spread of development into wilderness areas, encounters with feral dogs are growing. Cleo arrived with few clues,se threats, but surprisingly, Cleo, although she was very scared, neither growled nor bit.

The dog surprised us in every step of our experience with her. When I carried her to my car, she allowed it, then curled up in the corner of the seat and did not move during the entire trip home. My daughter and I had to pry her out of the car. She resisted passively, perhaps thinking that I would go away if she didn't move. She showed no signs of aggression. Once out of the car, she planted her feet firmly refusing to take a step. This defined my first objective: to let her know that no one was going to carry her and she would have to walk on a leash.

Attachment of a leash brought a typical response. She pulled back with all her strength and lied down. The dog must be kept on its feet if it is to walk and a leash and collar alone does not do it. We attached a harness to prevent her lying down. We had to master this before concentrating on anything else. Cleo <u>had</u> to walk on a leash; otherwise, I couldn't take her outside to relieve herself. I held the leash while my daughter held her up with the harness. It took only a few minutes for Cleo to understand what we wanted her to do. Soon, she walked easily with one person holding the leash and without the harness.

The fact that she showed strong passive resistance without any sign of aggression was surprising. Passive resistance commonly occurs in dogs that have never learned to work for anyone; those living basically alone or dogs who live with indulgent owners who spoil them constantly and nobody holds them accountable.

I moved to the next hurdle: convincing Cleo to relieve herself while walking her on a leash. Nature, after all, would call and she would not wet in the kennel. We walked and walked and walked for hours over a three day period before I discovered what she wanted, privacy. Females typically have this problem more than males. I discovered that if I took her to an area with tall grass, she would hide and take care of business while on a leash. What a relief for both of us.

She did not solicit any human attention or show any aggressive behavior, although, I remained keenly aware of the possibility. When I tried to get her out of her kennel, she crouched in the corner terrified of letting me touch her. As I often do with fearful dogs, I left a leash attached to her collar so I didn't have to reach around her neck and make her feel even more trapped. It is important to talk. If you are silent, animals think that you are trying to sneak up on them and it makes them very suspicious. I keep my voice low and speak slowly and calmly. I begin verbally assuring her that I am coming even before I get to her kennel. As I walk into the kennel building, I am calmly saying "Hi Cleo, how are you doing today? Do you want to go for a walk"? I open the kennel gate and squat down to pick up the end of her leash. I am very aware of keeping my body posture in a very non-threatening position. I lower my body and turn slightly away from her. For my own safety, I do not get on my knees. I need to remain on my feet so I can move quickly if needed. I am also careful to only give very short eye contact. All my movements are slow, <u>but not tentative</u>. If I act nervous, she will become even more concerned. I walked Cleo outside. Because of my confidence, she felt comfortable enough to come with me.

Now, it was on the classroom. When I entered the classroom full of students for the first time, Cleo looked for ways to make a speedy departure. However, she had to stay if I entertained any hope of socializing her. The compassionate. Students offered her tempting treats which she cautiously accepted. Within a couple of weeks, she romped with other dogs in the room. I the students were sitting in their chairs, she would accept pets and treats, but only if she came to them. She was still no domesticated.

After three weeks of training and many victories, one of the students placed Cleo in her kennel without properly latching the gate. Being a natural opportunist, Cleo took advantage of this and headed for the abundant brush and trees that surround my rural home. Anxiously, I began searching and calling for her. I thought I heard something move about a hundred yards away. When I looked, I saw Cleo peering through the blades of grass silently watching me. I felt that any move toward her would cause her to run and revert to her feral habits. Knowing she felt more relaxed around other dogs, I went to the kennel and got another foster dog with which Cleo enjoyed playing with before. Returning to the field with the dog, I knelt down with my back to Cleo and began to play with the other dog, petting it and acting as if we were having the time of our lives. I could sense Cleo creeping closer. Finally, she came close enough for me to reach slowly back, without turning around to look at her and take hold of her collar. When I felt I had a firm grip, I took in a long deep breath. I truly had not known if I would ever touch that collar again. I praised her thoroughly and both dogs got extra playtime in my training room. I wanted Cleo to know she had made the right decision.

We all grew very attached to this magnificent animal. Who would have guessed that a dog that had lived in the wild so long could have such a gentle temperament? After about a month in training, a wonderful family with other dogs and a securely fenced yard adopted her.

I last heard that she was becoming quite social and settling into her domestic life. Cleo had enriched all of our lives.

### *Is your dog aggressive only toward men or children?*

It is not unusual for a dog to show aggression toward a strange man verses a woman. Normally this is because they feel intimidated. Not that the man is trying to intimidate the dog, but in the dog world the male is usually more dominant and the leader of the pack. This may cause the dog to be more respectful of a male. Often dogs will obey the adult male in the house better than the female. Men are larger and have a deeper growl sound to their voice, which can sound much more serious than the voice of most women and children.

To help your dog overcome their fear of men, follow the previous steps on building your dog's confidence. Also, have a man be the only one to feed, pet and take for walks. If the dog gets all its needs met by women, it does not have any reason to socialize with men.

Dogs are often afraid of children if they have not grown up around them. Children move fast, are unpredictable and have high-pitched voices that sound much like an animal in trouble. Children can take some getting use to. Dogs, like people, can be afraid of what they don't understand. They also don't know how they are supposed to treat these little creatures. Are they to correct them as they would young puppies or respect them as human adults?

You can help your dog out by letting it study children from afar. Take your dog to a play area, but keep it on the outside edge, not too close to the kids playing. Let your dog watch and study these creatures without feeling threatened by them. Do not allow kids to come and pet your dog. I have seen owners hold their breath praying that their dog does not bite the approaching child. Just tell the children that your dog is afraid and they should stay away. If the situation appears comfortable, the child can drop a treat for your dog. You should also follow the previous steps on building your dog's confidence. Be sure to use a muzzle if you do not trust your dog. Do not risk anyone getting hurt. The muzzle will help everyone to relax.

If the children are in your home, do not take chances. If you are worried that your dog may bite, confine it in an area away from the children. If it appears safe, you can tie your dog in the room and tell the children to leave the dog alone and stay away. With you supervising you can have the children drop treats for your dog. If you are not sure about what your dog will do, play it safe and keep the kids away. Also, muzzle if needed.

### *Has your dog recently had puppies, been in season, or been bred?*

Hormones can drastically affect your dog's behavior. Males and females can become aggressive when hormones are high. You can avoid this problem by spaying or neutering your pet. If you are showing and/or breeding, be especially careful not to let your guard down during breeding times and when puppies are involved. Even the friendliest dog can bite if they think they are protecting their puppies.

When a female is in season near an un-neutered male, it can cause both dogs to be very stressed. Often they don't even eat. Only one thing is on their minds and nothing else is important to them.

Females can go through a false pregnancy even if they have not bred. They think they are pregnant and having puppies. Two months after they have been in season they may start nesting and even go so far as to adopt a stuffed animal or slipper as their new litter. They can become just as protective of their adopted family as if they actually had real puppies. As you can see, aggression may still occur even though there are no real puppies.

If you have unaltered pets, you must pay attention to their hormone changes and take precautions. Do not let strangers around them during breeding and delivery times. The first three days after a dog has delivered puppies she is not herself. If aggression should occur during this time, the owners are at fault for allowing people to stress her. The aggression should go away once the puppies are gone. Usually, the mom will settle down after the first three weeks.

### *Do your dogs parents or littermates have any aggression problems?*

You would be amazed at some of the behavior traits that can pass genetically. Sometimes it is serious behavior problems and other times just silly little antics. Genetic behavior can come from the mother, father or grandparents.

Aggression problems can be genetic. Many pet owners are not aware that their fluffy little puppy might have the same biting issues its father or mother had. If you don't like what temperaments you see in the parents, don't take one of the puppies.

If some of your dog's siblings show signs of aggression, it is likely that there is a genetic problem. If it is genetic you must be very careful. The aggression may be there to stay and what you do depends on the seriousness of the problem.

I realize that many of you did not have the luxury of meeting both parents or knowing any of the siblings, so you can never be totally sure if you are dealing with genetic aggression. If you do know the breeder, be sure to contact the breeder and find out all you can about the temperaments of the parents, grandparents and siblings. This will also help the breeder make a better choice on whom to breed the next time.

# Chapter Four

## *Does your dog have <u>displaced or redirected aggression</u>?*

    I give this question its own chapter because it involves aggression toward animals, but often results in biting people. Displaced or redirected aggression is very common with dogs that are aggressive to other dogs. This type of dog gets so revved up and frustrated when it can't get to the animal it wants to attack that it will grab whatever it can get its mouth on. At this moment it is often not even aware of who or what it is biting. This action is very common in terriers, but can be seen in any breed. Because the dog is not rational at this point, it is usually not a training issue. The training must come into place before the dog becomes riled in order to prevent the frenzied behavior from starting in the first place. This is not easy!

*The seriousness of displaced aggression is demonstrated in the following true story.*

## Classy

The plea had been coming in my email for several days now asking for a foster home for a male Belgian Malinois. I was assured he was gentle, friendly, trainable and non-aggressive. Keep in mind that Belgian Malinois are often used as police dogs and are what I consider a high-powered dog. This dog's parents were indeed working police dogs.

Although Classy really interested me, he was living a thousand miles away and I didn't know how I would get him. The Belgian Malinois rescue had saved him from the animal shelter and was working on finding him a suitable home, but he needed a place to live in the meantime.

When I sent my offer to house him if he could be delivered to me, I was suddenly thrown into the unfamiliar world of animal transport. As involved in dogs as I have been for the last seventeen years, I was totally unaware of the behind-the-scenes moving of animals performed by the many volunteers in order to save them from euthanasia and placing them in caring homes. My email was instantly filled with times, dates, places and connections. These people execute an awesome endeavor; the only reward is knowing that they have helped an innocent animal find a comfortable place to live out its life. I drove the last two hour leg of Classy's journey with the added assignment to deliver a kitten to cat rescue on my way back home.

I intercepted Classy in a store parking lot. As he peeled himself out of the crate he traveled in, I was instantly in awe of the striking presence and beauty of this dog. The person who delivered him explained that Classy didn't get along with one of the other male dogs in her car, so she had to put him in the crate for this leg of his trip. With Classy on leash in one hand, I was handed the kitten in a small crate for my other hand.

Once Classy notice the kitten he flipped into instant attack mode nearly knocking the crate out of my hand. I quickly handed the crate back and pulled the hysterically barking Classy behind a car so he could no longer see the kitten. This did not stop the frenzy. He dug all four feet into the blacktop, effectively using all his muscles, trying to get back to that crate while still barking furiously. What had I gotten myself into? After a few minutes he settled down and I loaded him into a crate in my car and placed the kitten up front were Classy could not see it. The rest of the trip was uneventful.

Classy was an awfully easy dog to love. He was gorgeous and pleasant to everyone; even strange men and little children were welcomed with a calm, wagging tail. He had the ability to display a relaxed confidence without being cocky. It was easy to forget the e-mail that claimed that he had fought with an intact male Bouvier at one of the over night stays during his trip to me. Even the kitten incidence seemed unimportant and distant.

This extremely athletic dog could easily clear an eight foot fence making it difficult to confine him. He escaped only to search for the closest person to hang out with.

Classy socialized well with my own dogs and the dogs in my boarding kennel, except for the two bratty pugs. These feisty little dogs really annoyed this otherwise mellow creature. As I casually walked Classy past the fenced pugs that were barking in an aggressive and challenging manner, Classy turned ferocious. He went for them as he did with the kitten. It took all my strength to hold him back. As I held tightly to the slip leash Classy barked and bit into the air in frustration, since he could not reach the pugs. This was the first time I felt uncomfortable with him. Could he have a displaced aggression problem, I wondered. It was too hard to believe of such a wonderful dog.

I continued to teach this untrained dog some basic obedience and train him to stay within an invisible fence, since no normal fence would restrain him. All was moving along very encouragingly. As we (my eight year old grandson, my own Belgian Sheepdog and Pomeranian) walked around the fence line showing Classy the boundary, my grandson picked up my Pomeranian. As the Pomeranian squirmed in his arms, Classy suddenly lunged for them aggressively. Fortunately, I still had a firm hold of his leash and stopped his assault. I instructed my grandson to put the dog down and when he did, Classy was totally fine with both of them. It appeared that when he saw the small wiggling animal he thought it was a cat. What would have happened if I did not have the leash in my hand? I don't want to know.

Since these incidents happened weeks apart, it was easy to make excuses and forgive the improper behavior because he was so exceptionally well behaved otherwise.

The day came that I wanted to walk Classy past the unruly pugs again. He needed to learn some self control, even if the little dogs didn't have any. It was time to use the obedience training that he had learned. The plan was to take one step toward the pugs, make Classy sit, stay and look at me and not them. I would praise him and then take one more step. The first step went according to plan. He sat straight looking me right in the eye, not at the other dogs. I praised him thoroughly and began one more small step. Half way through the step, Classy lunged past me so fast and strong I thought he might have actually gotten a hold of one of the pugs through the fence. In his furious frenzy, he was biting anything within reach, including me. I was shocked to feel a firm chomp on my left knee. Blood ran down my leg as I struggled to calm Classy and get him away from the Pugs. He turned it off as fast as he turned it on. He sat looking me straight in the eye just as if he were ready to continue his lesson as calmly as he had been when we started. Tears formed, I knew what the bite meant to Classy's hope of finding a home. Placing a dog into a home is a very important responsibility. People trust me and the dog rescues to be honest and not offer them a potentially dangerous dog; plus there are legal ramifications too.

    I added up all the warning signs. They could no longer be ignored or justified. I have the scars to remind me. All who took part in his rescuing process were involved in the decision of what to do now. I was thankful that it was me who was bitten and that I had not placed him with a family that may have taken him to the park with barking Pugs. Could this dog be a stay-at-home dog? Remember a fence would not hold him. The invisible fence is not a hundred percent reliable. True displaced aggression is very serious and obedience training cannot correct it, however, obedience training may be used to prevent an incident from occurring. Life is not always predictable!

## When Friendly Dogs Bite

    Many hours of phone calls all came to the same conclusion; it is not right to place an unsafe dog and the reliability was much too high. I had to follow the advice that I would had given other dog owners in this same position. Tearfully I said good-bye to Classy, who was truly a friendly dog that bit.

# Chapter five

## How can you choose a safe dog?

I would love to be able to give you some guaranteed steps to take so you can adopt a completely safe, non-aggressive pet for your family. Unfortunately, you can't always be sure, but I can give you some red flags to watch out for when considering adopting a dog.

***You may not want to adopt a dog if it shows any of the behaviors listed below:***

- Aggression problems in the parents or littermates.
- A dog who is fearful of strangers.
- Any dog who tenses up when people get around its food, bones, toys or anything it has stolen.
- Any aggression toward other dogs.

# When Friendly Dogs Bite

- **Growling, snapping, or baring its teeth at anyone for any reason.**

What you are looking for is a dog that is confident, happy and friendly to people and other animals. The dog should approach you with its tail wagging and face almost smiling just to be near you. It should invite petting, take a treat from you and when you walk away it should want to follow you. If it has a toy and you reach for it, the dog should gently release it to you.

I have heard a variety of reasons why people were attracted to the puppy that they picked from the litter. Don't be fooled as some of the following people were.

One family picked their puppy because they thought his independence was endearing. When they went to see the litter, the breeder opened the door and out ran the hoard of mix breed puppies. One stood out because he ran right past the prospective puppy buyers, off into the field and paid them no attention. Thinking this dog was special they took it home. When then came to me for help, they were having problems with coming and respect which was no surprise to me.

Another family wanted a quiet dog, so they picked the puppy that didn't come out of the whelping box. It just remained tucked into the corner. They were impressed with how quiet and calm this puppy was so they took it home. They came to me because this puppy was having confidence problems and was becoming a fear biter. This puppy had obviously been hiding in the corner because it was very afraid.

When the six-month-old Dalmatian puppy came to me, it walked into the room tense, growling with its hackles up. It would not come near me and did not stop growling as it hugged the wall. When I asked the owners what this puppy was like when they picked it out of the litter, they said that it hid behind the sofa growling and it took a half hour before they could even touch it. When I asked why they took this puppy, they replied that it was the cutest one.

My own sister came very close to choosing the wrong puppy for her, because she thought she wanted a female. The male was obviously a much better temperament for her. The male stayed with us playing and happy. The female ran away and would not come when we coaxed her. When she asked my advice I convinced her that it is much better to have a male with a good personality than a female with some problem behaviors. Fourteen years later she is still very happy to be living with this wonderful male dog.

*When going to look at a dog or puppy to adopt, be prepared to walk away without one if you don't like <u>everything</u> you see.*

- **Do not settle for a puppy just because you are there and the puppies are so cute.**
- **Do your homework, check out the breed and the breeder.**
- **Do not take the dominant puppy in the litter.**
- **Many times the runt of the litter is much more of a handful than most people realize. That puppy needs to be tough to survive.**
- **Puppies in a litter will have some squabbles as they work out their pecking order and learn**

## When Friendly Dogs Bite

proper dog etiquette, but if one of the puppies appears to be overly aggressive, picking on one puppy after another, be careful. This could be a sign of some very dominant behavior and a dog with aggression problems.

- Pick up the puppies; handle their feet, mouths and bodies. Roll them over gently in your arms and see how they react. A little mouthing and squirming is acceptable, but beware of growling and biting tantrums.

- If at all possible meet the parents of the puppies. If you don't like their temperaments don't take a puppy.

- Beware of puppy mills. If you buy from a pet store or order a dog off the internet you have a very good chance that you are supporting a puppy mill. A good breeder will check out the person purchasing their precious puppy. You must qualify to own the puppy in more ways than just having the proper amount of funds.

Remember the puppy or dog should come up to you happy with tail wagging. If you walk away it should want to follow you. If you are not sure which dog or puppy to adopt or you already did pick one and now you are having some aggression problems, check your area for an experienced behaviorist/trainer to help you.

# Chapter 6

## *How can you prevent a dog from biting you or your child?*

The dog is not always totally responsible for biting. Often it is from not understanding canines that gets people into trouble. Humans frequently don't follow the canine rules and in the dogs mind these people need to be educated. The dog gives a corrective snap, many times not even intending on making contact, but humans are just too slow at getting out of the way. The bite occurs. You can prevent this by knowing what not to do before the bite happens.

If a dog doesn't like what is happening they have three choices: they can tolerate it, they can leave or they can tell you to go away by growling, barring teeth, snapping or biting. Some dogs give lots of warnings that they are uncomfortable with what is happening and sometimes people listen. Children don't know what these warnings mean and often continue with what they are doing, resulting in a bite. Other dogs skip the warning and get right to the point, promptly chomping into the annoying person.

*Following the steps below should eliminate many of the unfortunate dog bites. Children should follow all these steps even with their own dogs, as many children are bitten by the dogs they live with.*

- **Never think you can move faster than a dog.** If you think you move fast enough to save yourself from getting bitten, you are wrong. If you don't get bitten, chances are the dog was not really trying to make contact. The snap was just intended to get you to stop what you were doing. I would guess that it worked. If you have witnessed an actual bite, you would see how fast it happens. I have videos of a dog biting and you have to play it in slow motion to see the bite happen.

- **Don't think that your child will be safe from a dog bite because you are close by and keeping an eye on them.** You must <u>prevent</u> your child from annoying the dog, do not think that you can stop the dog if it tries to bite. Think avoidance.

- **Never hug a dog that you don't live with.** A dog must know and trust you before it is comfortable being hugged. Some dogs never like it, but learn to tolerate. It is so important to teach your children this rule because when a child hugs a dog, the child's face is right in the line of fire if the dog snaps.

- **Never assume that because a dog has met you a couple of times it will remember you and accept you into its pack.** Dogs often need time to get comfortable with strangers. The canine definition of a stranger is anyone outside of the dogs pack.

- **Never run away from a dog or scream in fear.** The drive to chase something running is very strong in the canines. It will bring out the "chase down and catch" instinct, especially if there are two or more dogs.

- **If you are afraid, stay still.** Don't give the dog an excuse to bite you. Most dog won't bite someone just for standing still.

- **If a strange dog approaches you, making you feel uncomfortable, you can tell it in a firm voice to go away.** Sound like you are confident that you belong there and the dog needs to leave you alone. Many dogs know the word "no," so feel free to use it. It has often been stated that you must appear to be very submissive with no eye contact when challenged by an approaching dog. I have found it to be much more effective if I confront the dog straight on with firm eyes and voice. I do not yell, but I firmly tell the dog to, "Go home!" I am careful not to swing my arm out and point. This may make the dog think I am going to hit it.

- **Respect a dog that is eating or chewing on something.** Never allow children around dogs that are eating or chewing. Why take chances? Just don't do it!

- **Never leave children alone with dogs.** I have talked with many parents whose children have been bitten

## When Friendly Dogs Bite

and when I asked exactly what happened they couldn't tell me, because they weren't there and didn't see the incident. Had the parent been in sight, they might have avoided the bite.

- **Always ask before petting a strange dog.** Then only pet, don't lean into their face.

- **If a strange dog backs away from you don't pet it!**

- **Leave sleeping dogs alone.** Do not startle or move a dog that is sleeping or resting.

- **Never swing your hands or feet at a dog.** You do not want to look as though you are trying to hit or kick a dog

Made in the USA
Lexington, KY
05 January 2013